THE MORAL UNIVERSITY

Maurice R. Berube
and Clair T. Berube

ROWMAN & LITTLEFIELD PUBLISHERS, INC.
Lanham • Boulder • New York • Toronto • Plymouth, UK

Published by Rowman & Littlefield Publishers, Inc.
A wholly owned subsidiary of The Rowman & Littlefield Publishing Group, Inc.
4501 Forbes Boulevard, Suite 200, Lanham, Maryland 20706
http://www.rowmanlittlefield.com

Estover Road, Plymouth PL6 7PY, United Kingdom

British Library Cataloguing in Publication Information Available

Library of Congress Cataloging-in-Publication Data

Berube, Maurice R.
  The moral university / Maurice R. Berube and Clair T. Berube.
    p. cm.
  Includes bibliographical references and index.
  ISBN 978-0-7425-6107-6 (cloth : alk. paper) — ISBN 978-0-7425-6108-3 (pbk. :
alk. paper) — ISBN 978-1-4422-0484-3 (electronic)
  1. Education, Higher—Moral and ethical aspects. 2. Moral education
(Higher) I. Berube, Clair T. II. Title.
  LB2324.B47 2010
  378'.014—dc22   2010004301

∞™ The paper used in this publication meets the minimum requirements of
American National Standard for Information Sciences—Permanence of Paper
for Printed Library Materials, ANSI/NISO Z39.48-1992.

Printed in the United States of America

THE MORAL UNIVERSITY

For our children

CONTENTS

ACKNOWLEDGMENTS

We gratefully acknowledge the participation of the following scholars: Bruce Wilshire, Jerome Karabel, Diane Ravitch, Arthur C. Danto, Henry Giroux, Michael Bèrubè, Jeffrey Glanz, James V. Koch, Roseanne Runte, Stanley Aronowitz, Peter Steinfels, Janet Lyon, Dana Heller, Philip Altbach, Sophie Body-Gendrot, and Francesca Gobbo.

1

THE MORAL UNIVERSITY

Are colleges and universities moral institutions? The thesis of this book is that they are, by their natures, and in varying measures. We will look at the best examples of the universities operating in a moral fashion toward students, faculty, community, and nation, and we will conclude with a profile of the exemplar moral university.

John Dewey, arguably the most important philosopher of education in the modern era, contended that education is moral and that the duty of educators is to develop that moral sense. In his small treatise, *Moral Principles in Education* (1909), Dewey argued that "the development of character is the end of all school work" and that teachers should see that "moral ideals" be developed "in persons."[1] Dewey perceived "a moral trinity of the school" whereby students would be imbued with "social intelligence, social power, and social interests."[2]

A classic text arguing for a moral component to education is British philosopher R. S. Peters's *Ethics and Education* (1970). Peters argues that the process of education is structured around ethical principles. He wrote that "educational issues should give rise to ethical questions is not a contingent matter. . . . 'Education' has notions such as 'improvement,' 'betterment,' and 'the passing on of what is worthwhile' built into it. That education must involve something of ethical value is, therefore, a matter of logical necessity."[3]

Peters's treatise examines the philosophy of education from various perspectives of education and equality, education and freedom, and education and democracy. He remarks that "the ethical foundation of 'equality' and 'fairness' may well seem more solid than those of the content of education."[4] On democracy, Peters argues that "as a way of life it represents an articulation in appropriate institutions of the fundamental principles of morality," thus "its ethical foundations have already been established."[5]

But there is no unanimity that universities are moral institutions. The eminent literary critic Stanley Fish, distinguished university professor of law at Florida International University, argues in his book *Save the World on Your Own Time* (2008) that the only thing that is a mandate of the university is intellectual development. "What exactly is the job of higher education?" Fish asks. His answer is clear:

> College and university teachers can (legitimately) do two things: (1) introduce students to bodies of knowledge [and] (2) equip those same students with the analytical skills . . . that will enable them to move confidently. . . . That's all there is to it, nothing more, nothing less.[6]

Another dissenter who stated that moral education is not the province of the university is John J. Mearsheimer, distinguished professor of political science at the University of Chicago. In 1997, he delivered the annual "Aims of Education" address to incoming freshman, declaring that "the university makes little effort to provide you with moral guidance."[7] Mearsheimer argued that the university is "a remarkably amoral institution."[8] He instructed that the faculty is "silent on the issue of morality" and that those classes "where you discuss ethics or morality" actually "do not exist" at the University of Chicago.[9]

And the former president of Harvard, Derek Bok, in his book *Our Underachieving Colleges* (2007), wonders whether "moral development should be merely an option for students or should it be an integral part of the curriculum?"[10] He ambivalently concludes that "it is time to address this question with the care and deliberation it deserves."[11]

THE HISTORY OF THE MODERN UNIVERSITY

The evolution of the modern university has progressed through three stages. First, there was the Cardinal Newman model, which stressed education for education's sake. Second was the rise of the German research university, and third, the American contribution—the service university—emerged. The moral university is a variant of the service university.

Newman's lectures—assembled in *The Idea of the University* (1873)—have been called "one of the educational and literary masterpieces of the Western world."[12] His message is that knowledge is "its own end."[13] The reason for a university, then, is to develop "intellectual excellence" divorced from any moral component, or as Newman scholar Frank M. Turner interprets it, "that excellence was not to be confused with moral transformation."[14]

The German research university that developed in the nineteenth century sought "content-neutral" knowledge. The research mode transformed the nature of the university into pure intellectual work. One subtext was the training and preparation of academic researchers with newly minted PhDs. This led to the creation of modern scholars as specialists. The German research university heralded the university as an end in itself, that the university was in fact the faculty. Students were necessary only as they took their place as junior scholars.

During the mid-nineteenth century, while Newman lectured and wrote and the German university was emerging, the American university was also changing. It was becoming a service-oriented university dealing with community and national needs. The breakthrough was the 1862 Land Grant Act, which enabled American universities to aid in the development of agriculture at a time when it was lagging and the Industrial Revolution was in full flower.

Twenty-five years later that service concept expanded. Smith College pioneered in settlement work with the poor Jews and Catholics in New York City. The college settlement movement grew and such universities as Chicago, Michigan, Northwestern, Wisconsin, Harvard, Butler, and Vassar joined in settlement work. That work varied from giving public baths, hymn singing, and providing thrift lessons to instilling social organizing skills. The assumption of the settlement movement was that universities must lead the way in social reform.

BRUCE WILSHIRE

Bruce Wilshire, a critic of the modern university and senior professor of philosophy at Rutgers, argues in his book *The Moral Collapse of the University* (1990) that "education is a moral enterprise and that the contemporary research university lacks moral direction."[15]

Wilshire holds out hope for the moral regeneration of the academy. He teaches a course entitled "Current Moral and Social Issues."[16] He declares that "the ethical responsibility of the individual professor is inescapable."[17] And the task before professors "if we would restore the university to its educational and moral course" is to "rethink what it means to be a human being."[18]

Wilshire cites the triad of "science, technology, and professionalism" that emerged from the nineteenth-century influence of German universities with their research agenda as determinants of the modern university.[19] In academia, the German example resulted in the development of "specialized fields—the model of science" that diminished the importance of a moral influence.[20] Moreover, he notes that "ethical beliefs and practices had been traditionally enmeshed for most with religious beliefs and practices, and when religion was separated from the official center of public life, it tended to take ethics with it."[21]

Two years later Edward LeRoy Long Jr. would take up Wilshire's challenge and contend in his book *Higher Education as a Moral Enterprise* (1992) that "higher education is fundamentally a moral enterprise that needs to be guided by commitments to what is morally right and fundamentally good."[22] The trick for administrators and faculty, according to Long, is to devise "policies and strategies" that are "crucial to the nurturing of a moral enterprise."[23]

In his classic study, *The Soul of the American University* (1993), George M. Marsden traces the development of the American university from one founded on evangelical Protestantism to one transformed into liberal Protestantism and eventually to secular morality. The turning point came with the rise of Darwin and evolutionary biology in the late nineteenth century. The modern university was born with a new scientific perspective but also with vestiges of a liberal religious orientation. By the 1960s, postmodernism was wedded to a naturalistic science orientation, and religious influences were nearly extinct.

With the emergence of the modern university at the turn of the nineteenth century, American universities were "integral parts of a religious-cultural heritage."[24] Harvard became the "flagship setting the pace for a national educational ideology."[25] At the turn of the century, Harvard enjoyed a golden age with such philosophers as William James, Josiah Royce, George Santayana, and Hugo Mustenberg on its faculty. In addition, Marsden points out that "Harvard was the first American school to feel the impact of the ideal presented by the rising eminence of the German universities."[26]

Marsden notes that "during this transitional era" at Harvard from religion to science, a "diversified effort" occurred to "fill the spiritual and moral void created by the demise of moral philosophy."[27] The social sciences demonstrated a "moral earnestness," as did history and the natural sciences, which were "seen as sacred expressions of moral integrity."[28] Indeed, even "the emerging fields of literature and the arts were especially conspicuous in taking over a spiritual and moral role."[29] Harvard had created a "new humanistic religion of humanity and high culture."[30] Harvard had "accentuated a theme that was apparent at other major universities as well."[31]

But the twentieth-century revelations of naturalistic science took their toil on religion as a perspective to be taken seriously. "Religious viewpoints," Marsden argues, "at least traditional ones, were considered both unscientific and socially disruptive."[32] Instead, "a unified and universal science would provide an objective basis for a unified society."[33]

ATTACK

Toward the end of the twentieth century, the academy became a target for the political right, which charged that the university had been captured by the political left. The first salvo came from Allan Bloom, from the University of Chicago, who decried the university as a captive of the social 1960s. In his best-selling book *The Closing of the American Mind* (1987), Bloom accuses students of believing that "truth is relative."[34] For these students "the relativity of truth is not a theoretical insight but a moral postulate."[35] Bloom argues that "the mythology of the sixties is the alleged superior moral 'concern' of the student," as evidenced by their participation in the civil rights and anti-Vietnam movements.[36] But Bloom concedes that "every educational system has a moral goal."[37]

Bloom's subtitle to the book is instructive: "How Higher Education Has Failed Democracy and Impoverished the Souls of Today's Students." What is Bloom's solution? Answer: restoring the canon and the "great books." He states that "the only serious solution is the one that is almost universally rejected: the good old Great Books approach, in which a liberal education means reading certain generally recognized classic texts."[38] Reading the classic texts, he argues, is a "special experience."[39]

Close on the heels of the Bloom attack was Roger Kimball's denunciation of the liberal professoriate in his book *Tenured*

Radicals (1990). Kimball accuses liberal professors, who he claims dominate the academy, of a "perverted moralism." He claims that this "moralism" emphasizes "gender-race-class" and defines "virtue" as whatever sexual, feminist, Marxist, racial, or ethnic agenda to which the particular critic has declared his allegiance."[40] Kimball dismisses this "moralism as unconvincing—it is preachably moralistic rather than genuinely concerned with moral issues."[41]

Another attack on professors was Charles J. Sykes's *ProfScam* (1988). Sykes charges that professors are "overpaid, grotesquely underworked" and that they had "abandoned their teaching responsibilities" to pursue "their own interests—research, academic politics, cushier grants."[42] He argues that liberal arts professors have an "obsession with trendy theory" and education professors are "poisoning the entire educational system."[43] His solution to the alleged problems in higher education is to abolish tenure and require teachers to teach and to "insist on a prescribed curriculum for underclassmen that would ensure that all students are exposed to the basic classics of Western thought"—in short, restoring the "canon."[44]

SOME OTHER OPINIONS

The authors conducted a small, purposeful survey regarding the question of whether a university should pursue a moral course. The sample included college presidents, a philosopher, an educational historian, a literary critic, a critical theorist, and an educational scholar and policy analyst. The consensus was that a university should be moral, although there were codicils on some of these affirmations.

Drew Gilpin Faust, Harvard University's first female president, declared in her inaugural speech on October 12, 2007, that the university was a moral institution. "Universities are uniquely a place of philosophers and scientists," she declared.[45] "It is urgent that we pose the questions of ethics and meaning that will enable

us to confront the human and the social and the moral signifi-
cance of our changing relationships with the natural world."[46]

Jerome Karabel, author of *The Chosen: The Hidden History of
Admission and Exclusion at Harvard, Yale, and Princeton* (2006)
says "writing a book called *The Moral University* sounds like a
wonderful idea."[47] He notes that he had always "assessed universities by the extent to which they live up to professed ideals."[48]
Arthur C. Danto, emeritus professor from Columbia, philosopher,
and art critic, agrees that "universities have a moral mission beyond and presupposed by the transmission of knowledge."[49] He
believes that the university must "begin with the moral weight
of truth itself, and the ethics of finding it, the responsibility of
fairness in considering testimony, and the respect owed to beliefs
other than our own."[50] Danto feels that "we live in terrible times
for truth, and the university derives a special importance as an
example of an institution that respects the truth and protects
truth and those who seek it."[51]

Educational historian Diane Ravitch of New York University,
author of *The Troubled Crusade* (1983), argues that "universities,
like other institutions, have an ethical obligation to act in a moral
way toward students, faculty, community and nation."[52] The
university, she contends, "must be accountable for its actions,
in other words, the institution must adhere to clear ethical and
moral standards."[53]

Critical theorist and author of *The University in Chains* (2007)
Henry Giroux of McMaster University believes that "pedagogy at
its best is about a political and moral practice" and that the university "as a democratic public sphere has a role it plays in pre-
supposing a society that is more just, democratic and free from
human suffering."[54] Literary critic Michael Bèrubè, Paterno Chair
in English at Penn State and author of *What's Liberal about the
Liberal Arts?* (2006), finds the question of whether a university is
moral "a large question" but suggests that universities "should try
to educate students so as to enhance their abilities and capacities
to engage in civil life and civil society."[55]

Educational scholar and policy analyst Jeffrey Glanz, the Silverstein Chair in Professional Ethics and Values at Yeshiva University, argues that universities should "help students develop the critical thinking necessary to choose for themselves what is moral and what is not."[56] Although he does not "advocate that a university take a moral stance," he feels "that it does by the very fact of encouraging students to think critically to reach sound, reasonable moral solutions to ethical dilemmas."[57]

James V. Koch, former president of Old Dominion University and author of *Presidential Leadership*, contends that "universities, even public universities, should be operated from the vantage point of moral values unless those values conflict with state laws or the institution's regulations."[58] His successor at Old Dominion, Roseanne Runte, agrees that the university "must act in a moral fashion" since "it is not like other institutions."[59]

Nevertheless, some respondents had reservations. James V. Koch went to the heart of the matter, declaring that "the basic problem nationally is whose moral standard we are talking about? Mine, Pat Robertson's, Bill Clinton, or whose? There is little agreement about what is moral or immoral."[60]

Michael Bèrubè could not see how "university departments have an obligation to be moral."[61] He asks "how does a college act morally toward a nation?"[62] Lawrence Kohlberg's research on morality provides useful insight. There are levels of moral understanding and conduct. Consequently, universities vary considerably in their pursuit of a moral character.

CONCLUSION

We examine a number of critical moral issues regarding students and the university. First, we analyze the attempts to develop moral reasoning among students. We discuss the university's responsibility to provide a safe environment in the wake of the Virginia Tech shootings. We also discuss the need to deal with sexual harassment from faculty or fellow students. And we examine the need for a civil collegiate society that does not require speech codes.

What is the responsibility of the college administration to the faculty and the faculty to the institution? We examine safety measures, faculty-controlled curriculum, gender equity, sexual harassment, and substance abuse, among other key issues. We also examine the role that universities play in their communities and their impact on national policy.

THE MORAL
CURRICULUM

One direct way in which universities can move toward a moral stance is by offering courses that involve moral reasoning. Since the 1960s, more of these types of courses have appeared in professional schools and undergraduate curricula. This phenomenon was a response to the 1960s controversies regarding race and gender. Nevertheless, there is no faculty consensus on the need to require courses on moral reasoning.

The professional schools are ahead on this issue. Schools of law, medicine, and business now mandate courses on practical ethics. Undergraduate liberal arts schools have yet to catch up. As mentioned in the chapter 1, no less a person than the former president of Harvard—Derek Bok—would conclude that the issue of requiring moral reasoning courses resulted in "ambivalence" for administrators despite "polls that show both students and faculty desire such courses."[1]

Elite business colleges have set the standard for moral reasoning courses. At Harvard Business School, students have devised "the MBA oath," a pledge to "serve the greater good."[2] The pledge is for students to act ethically and submerge their "own narrow ambitions" for the welfare of others.[3] Almost 20 percent of the 2009 graduating class signed the pledge.

At Columbia Business School, students have an honor code stating that the students will "adhere to the principles of truth, integrity, and respect" and will not lie, cheat, or steal.[4] At the Wharton School of Business at the University of Pennsylvania, ethics classes have become so popular that the university increased faculty from two professors to seven for these courses that were "among the most popular at the school."[5]

Nevertheless, although these moral courses do not have a *profound* effect on college students, there are indications that they are of some benefit. According to Bok's research in his book *Our Underachieving Colleges* there are at best "grounds for believing that well-taught courses in practical ethics will tend to have at least a modest effect on behavior."[6]

Studies have indicated that moral reasoning courses can produce "modest overall" development in moral judgment.[7] A 1985 meta-analysis of fifty-five studies of "education intervention designed to stimulate development in moral judgment" showed positive influence.[8] A meta-analysis is a sophisticated analysis of a number of statistical studies to establish a trend. The authors of the meta-analysis tested various interventions involving upper-class high school students, college, and graduate students and adults. The authors conclude that the meta-analysis reveals that there is a positive outcome on the effects of moral reasoning courses.[9]

Subsequent studies regarding the effect of college on moral reasoning are mixed. Significantly higher scores for moral judgment were reported for ethics students on courses with explicit moral content by one team of researchers in 2008.[10] Other researchers did not reach the same conclusion.[11] Similarly, courses on diversity and social justice again were mixed in regard to the development of moral reasoning. The same researchers who found higher scores for moral content courses also found corresponding higher scores for diversity and social justice courses, whereas other researchers did not.[12] However, service learning courses and participation in community service did "facilitate the development of moral reasoning.[13]

A major study on moral reasoning was presented to the American Educational Research Association conference in 2009. The researchers—Matthew J. Mayhew, Tricia A. Seifert, and Ernest T. Pascarella—conducted a study on moral reasoning on 1,469 freshman students in nineteen institutions. They focused on "how transition plays a role in understanding college's impact on students."[14] They concluded that students in "moral transition"—that is, not having formed strong preferences—were "more developmentally ready" and "made significant gains in moral reasoning" with college content and educational practices of the instructor, such as intensive moral discussions in the classroom.[15] However, the college experience was not as morally effective for those students they term "consolidated students," who come into college with strongly held views.

Still, teaching ethics presents a difficult task. Robert J. Sternberg, dean of the School of Arts and Sciences at Tufts University, wonders "why it is hard to translate theory into practice, even after one has studied ethical leadership for several months?"[16] In an article in the *Chronicle of Higher Education*, Sternberg reveals how he presented seventeen "gifted" undergraduates in his leadership seminar with a scenario involving obtaining double compensation for a consulting trip. The response was lukewarm, leaving him to wonder "how hard it is to translate theories of ethics, even case studies, into practice."[17] He concludes that "colleges can produce students who are smart and knowledgeable but ethically challenged."[18]

HARVARD'S JUSTICE COURSE

One case study of an enormously popular moral reasoning course is Harvard's "Moral Reasoning 22," more commonly called "Justice" and taught by political scientist Michael Sandel. It is "one of Harvard's most popular courses" since its inception in 1980, and Sandel teaches it in the Sanders Theatre to an estimated 1,000 students.[19]

"Justice" enrolls "one in six Harvard undergrads" and they debate "inequality, tax policy, affirmative action, gay marriage, and abortion," among other topics.[20] Students read "canonical political theory texts," such as "Aristotle, Jeremy Bentham, John Stuart Mill, John Locke, John Rawls, and Robert Nozick."[21] The course has become a legend among its 14,000 Harvard alumni and spawned a twelve-episode documentary for PBS in fall 2009 entitled *Justice: What's the Right Thing to Do?* The course has been augmented by a tie-in book and a celebrated book tour.

Sandel, a graduate of Brandeis and Oxford, is described as a "man of the left or center-left" who nonetheless "makes a point of giving students with dissenting views a hearing."[22] His students form a constituency that provides "counterevidence to the theory (put forward by a federal judge and legal scholar Richard Posner, among others) that moral judgment doesn't change minds."[23]

The new prominence of justice promises that Sandel might "break through to a new level of intellectual influences."[24]

Sandel's companion book to the PBS series was also entitled *Justice: What's the Right Thing to Do?* In the book, Sandel grounds his contemporary examples of moral dilemmas in classic philosophical underpinnings. He posits three choices on moral conundrums: Jeremy Bentham's philosophy of the greatest good for the greatest number, Immanuel Kant's argument for individual rights, and John Rawls's rationale for social justice.[25]

Sandel concludes that "a politics of moral engagement" is necessary for the just person. He writes that "a politics of moral engagement is not only a more inspiring ideal than a politics of avoidance [but] it is also a more promising basis for a just society."[26]

Prior to the Civil War, colleges required a course in moral philosophy, usually taught by the college or university president, which served as the culminating academic experience. The course was comprised of a survey of ethical principles applied to topical issues of the day.

In the moral era, Lawrence Kohlberg and Carol Gilligan of Harvard pioneered moral development and moral reasoning courses at Harvard. In the 1950s Kohlberg began a fifteen-year study of boys and their moral development. He also founded the Center for Moral Development. Both he and Gilligan taught moral reasoning courses at Harvard.

Gilligan looked at the other side of the coin: the moral development of girls. In a classic study, *In a Different Voice: Psychological Theory and Women's Development* (1982), Gilligan discovered a different pattern of moral reasoning with girls. Whereas to Kohlberg's boys, moral problems were perceived to be like math problems with six stages of development, the highest being an ethic of justice, Gilligan perceived in her girls a pattern of care and a web of relationships. Gilligan's students did not respond in a linear fashion but perceived a context to moral issues that consisted of long-term solutions. For example, when asked the Immanuel Kant conundrum of what a poor person should do to obtain medicine for an extremely ill mate, the boys answered that the person should steal the medicine. Gilligan's girls replied that such an act would probably mean jail and the unavailability of the husband to respond when and if the wife becomes ill again. Both Kohlberg and Gilligan were highly influential and provoked controversy.

Gilligan now teaches as affiliated faculty in the School of Law at New York University. Along with a constitutional law professor, Gilligan co-teaches a yearlong course titled "Resisting Injustice."[27] The course description asks "why people resist injustice" and states that the course explores "the roots of ethical resistance," covering resistance in "sexual liberation, the civil rights movement, second wave feminism and gay rights."[28]

SOME OPINIONS

Bruce Wilshire thought the question of a required moral reasoning course for liberal arts students "completely straightforward and timely."[29] He feels that "a course in moral reasoning should be required" but that "it all depends on who does the teaching and how it's done."[30] Wilshire warned that if the course is "not tied into student's lives, into what really means something to them, then everyone just goes through the motions—another requirement."[31]

Jeffrey Glanz "most definitely" believes that a moral reasoning course should be required in undergraduate liberal arts colleges.[32] But he adds that "a course by itself does not ensure a deepening of moral values and ethical behavior."[33] This moral component, he contends, must "permeate the school organization and interactions with the community."[34] Moreover, Glanz argues, "educational leaders must serve as moral exemplars."[35]

Michael Bèrubè feels that a moral reasoning course should be required in a liberal arts curriculum but worries that "you'll need a whole raft of philosophy faculty to teach it" and that they would "probably oppose it" since it "wouldn't give them the chance to teach anything else."[36] Stanley Aronowitz, distinguished professor of cultural studies at City University of New York and author of *The Knowledge Factory*, was also in agreement. However, Aronowitz was concerned about possible conservative bias. "If the deck is stacked, I say no," he comments. But "if the course raises controversies over war, for example, yes, it would be valuable."[37]

Diane Ravitch opposes a *separate* course on moral reasoning. Instead, she advocates that moral reasoning "be embedded in all courses—in science, mathematics, history, literature."[38] She adds that "there is an ethical dimension in all these fields that should be the heart of instruction."[39]

Peter Steinfels, co-director of Fordham University's Center for Religion and Culture and former religion columnist for the *New York Times*, opines that "universities have a special responsibility to teach morals, especially to undergraduates."[40] But, like Ravitch, he believes that moral reasoning should be imbued in all the course offerings rather than offered as a separate course. He is especially concerned that religious schools maintain their "distinctive religious character" yet adhere to "academic freedom in their inquiry."[41]

Opposition to the teaching of moral reasoning in a classroom setting comes from Stanley Fish. In his book, *Save the World on Your Own Time* (2008), Fish argues that

> Teachers cannot . . . fashion moral character. . . . But if they do that they will be practicing without a license and in all likelihood doing a bad job at a job they shouldn't be doing at all.
>
> I should acknowledge upfront that mine is a minority view. . . . My contention is that academization is the only thing that should be happening in the classroom. . . . This position [is] sometimes called derisively the Ivory Tower position.[42]

INDOCTRINATION

As some scholars have pointed out, there is a thin line between moral development in academia and indoctrination toward a particular political agenda. In a recent case, Derek Bok, in *Our Underachieving Colleges*, erroneously attacks critical theorist Henry Giroux for raising "the specter of indoctrination."[43] Bok dismisses Giroux's charge that "professors should try to change society for the better by engaging their students with 'critical pedagogy'" that "seeks to celebrate responsible action and strategic risks as part of an ongoing struggle and 'which reflects' a shared conception of social justice."[44]

Bok appears uncomfortable with Giroux's leftist credentials as a neo-Marxist scholar. Bok's specific complaint is that Giroux cites as "official villains" corporations that "have been given too much power in this society and hence the need for educators and others to address the threat this poses to all facets of public life."[45] Bok eschews Giroux's "specific political agenda," which he finds "deeply unsettling."[46] Bok approves the theory of moral development in academia but shies away from the actual application of moral ideals.

Giroux responded to us in an e-mail, saying that Bok "seems to believe that if you connect matters of critique with a call for modes of agency that takes seriously matters of social responsibility you are somehow indoctrinating people."[47] He adds that "stressing that students should be responsible for the democracies they live in is not the same thing as telling them what political positions to advocate."[48]

How does one avoid indoctrination? In *What's Liberal about the Liberal Arts?* (2007), Michael Bèrubè, then teaching at the University of Illinois at Champaign-Urbana, identified himself as a "campus liberal" teaching mostly conservative students in the Midwest.[49] He comments that although he is "open to all manner of reasonable challenges" to his beliefs he "inevitably" comes "into conflict with certain kinds of conservatives" who display a "moral mist" or opacity.[50] These students find that "certain positions are tacitly understood to be more virtuous than others."[51] The trick is to have an open classroom, with professor and students ready to discuss all points of view. *In Beyond the Culture Wars* (1992), Gerald Graff argues that a professor should not shy away from "teaching the conflicts" but should teach in a manner that exposes students "to an endless series of different positions."[52]

THE PRIVATE ELITE UNIVERSITIES

Today, Harvard requires moral reasoning courses in its core program for undergraduates. The courses aim to "give students some practice in thinking critically about moral and ethical problems."[53] Henry Rosovsky, former Harvard dean, describes the core moral reasoning course as follows:

> Instruction in moral reasoning in the Core Curriculum does not teach or preach a specific morality of philosophy. . . . Our aim is "to discuss significant and recurrent questions of choice and values that arise in human experience"—moral issues that are shared

by many religious and philosophical conceptions of mankind and that cannot be resolved by appeal to emotion.[54]

In addition to the core program, there exist four courses on moral development. In the philosophy department, there are three separate courses in moral reasoning, including one titled "Moral Reasoning and Social Protest." In the psychology department there is a laboratory course on moral cognition.[55]

At Stanford, the moral reasoning courses are found in the philosophy department's catalog, in the joint major in philosophy and religion. In the philosophy department, there is a "Moral and Political Philosophy" course required of all majors. In the joint program, there exist the courses "Ethical Reasoning" and "Ethics and Value Theory."[56]

Duke University has exercised the option of requiring a moral component as part of all courses in the core curriculum for undergraduates. An emphasis on ethical inquiry is required as part of four areas of knowledge in the core—arts/literature, civilization/philosophy, social sciences, and nature sciences.[57]

THE PUBLIC UNIVERSITIES

The University of Wisconsin–Madison requires ethnic studies courses in its general education program for undergraduates. This emphasis seeks to "understand culture and contributions of persistently marginalized racial or ethnic groups."[58] In the philosophy department, a required course is "Introductory Ethics," which examines "the nature of moral problems and ethical theory."[59]

The University of California, Berkeley, suffuses its curriculum for undergraduates with a "moral and historic compass" in order to "distinguish good from evil, justice from injustice."[60] At the University of Texas, the philosophy department offers "Contemporary Moral Problems," a course that examines "problems of abortion, sexual morality, capital punishment, and pornography and hate speech."[61] A paper is required on "social justice historical figures," whereby the student chooses to write about "individuals who worked or are working for social justice."[62] One of the required texts is Catherine Marshall and Maricela Oliva's *Leadership for Social Justice* (2005). Additional readings include Paulo Freire's classic *Pedagogy of the Oppressed* (1971). Recommended readings include the work of three critical theorists: Michael Apple, Henry Giroux, and Peter McLaren.

THE RELIGIOUS UNIVERSITIES

Religious institutions are the exception. These universities formally require courses with moral values embedded in their philosophy, theology, and even social science courses. As a student at Fordham University (a Jesuit Catholic University) in the 1950s, I (Maurice) took philosophy courses dealing with morality. Clair, at Virginia Wesleyan, a Methodist college, in the 1980s took a required history of religion course.

Today Fordham requires of all sophomores in its core curriculum a course entitled "Philosophical Ethics." The course description cites study of the great moral philosophers such as Plato, Locke, and Kant. Topics include ethics and feminism, suicide, war, and censorship. Also, a critical reasoning course is offered to undergraduate students with a heavy moral bent that tilted toward questions of social justice.[63]

Virginia Wesleyan has also expanded its moral reasoning courses. There now exist five courses on the subject: "Contemporary Moral Issues," "Types of Ethical Theory," "Ethics and Health Care," "Environmental Ethics," and "Critical Reasoning."[64]

Loyola University has also progressed from the two ethics course required in the early 1960s, when Peter Steinfels attended. Today, Loyola offers a core curriculum that has a required ethics component for all undergraduates. The students can choose among courses such as "Health Care and Ethics," "Business Ethics," "Education and Ethics," and "Environmental Ethics."

The syllabus for Education and Ethics cites three areas of study to guide "the activity of teaching."[65] The first, "philosophical knowledge and ethics," requires readings in Aristotle, Kant, Mill, and Nel Noddings. There, ethical theories are discussed that "describe moral life and direct moral decision-making."[66] The second area of study, "skills developed," concentrates on "critical thinking skills and ethical awareness and decision making." The third area, "values," emphasizes "promoting justice, promoting civic engagement or leadership."[67]

Regent University, a conservative Christian university under the leadership of the televangelist Pat Robertson, distributes its moral reasoning courses throughout the undergraduate curriculum. For example, in its psychology department, the intention is to present a "Christ centered approach to psychology theory and practice."[68] Also, the same approach is applied to "government and politics" area of study.[69]

CONCLUSION

Our sample clearly indicates increased interest in moral reasoning courses. Some universities have such courses required in a core curriculum or general education program as entry-level introductory courses. Some of these courses widen subject matter by including questions of social justice. Nevertheless, this small sample presents a positive picture of evolving moral concern among universities. We can extrapolate from the sample that a model curriculum should both emphasize the great moral philosophers and apply their principles to contemporary social justice problems.

LEADERSHIP FOR SOCIAL CHANGE

Increasingly, universities have offered courses and programs involving social change. Administrators view these efforts as part of their mission to connect with the real world and leave the ivory tower. Nonetheless, these courses and programs have been subject to attacks from conservatives who perceive "social change" as code for "politically liberal." A case in point was the controversy surrounding an accrediting agency for school of education programs.

THE NATIONAL COUNCIL OF ACCREDITATION FOR TEACHER EDUCATION (NCATE) AND "SOCIAL CHANGE"

The nation's premier accrediting agency for colleges of education has been the National Council of Accreditation for Teacher Education (NCATE). Recently, NCATE *required* colleges of education to prepare education students with "dispositions" that would be "guided by beliefs and attitudes related to values, caring, fairness, honesty, responsibility, and *social justice*."[1]

The problem is that some teachers and conservative groups interpret social justice as meaning indoctrination of liberal political ideas. Stephen Balch, head of the conservative National Association of Scholars, considers the phrase "ideologically freighted."[2] Greg Lukianoff, president of the Foundation for Individual Rights in Education (FIRE), terms the phrase a "vague and politically loaded recommendation."[3] Lukianoff goes on to say that "there is no way an education school can evaluate a student's commitment to 'social justice' without evaluating his or her politics."[4] Both groups intended to testify before the U.S. Department of Education's evaluations of accrediting agencies to demand that NCATE not receive renewal approval. But before they could testify, NCATE president Arthur Wise announced that the accrediting agency would remove the phrase "social justice" from their standards for accrediting colleges of education.

Wise would comment that NCATE does not seek "thought control" and that the standards "do not expect or require institutions to attend to any particular political or social ideologies."[5] Some professors consider the change a cave-in to politically conservative groups.

MAURICE'S EXPERIENCE WITH SOCIAL CHANGE

I was a social activist for two decades before becoming a part of the academic community. In the 1950s, I was both an editor and organizer for Association of Catholic Trade Unionists (ACTU). ACTU was engaged in fighting Mafia unions that oppressed poor Puerto Rican workers. Subsequently, in the 1960s, I was an editor and organizer for the teachers' union in New York City, the United Federation of Teachers AFL-CIO. I was also a member of the Socialist Party (SP) and wrote about education issues for the SP's publications.

By the late 1960s, I was a member of a university-based think tank, the Institute for Community Studies, that both conducted studies in education and served as a major supporter of the community control movement in education, which was a part of the black power phase of the civil rights movement.

By the 1970s, I was a teacher at Queens College in New York in the Urban Studies Department, an offshoot of the Institute for Community Studies. Marilyn Gittell, the political scientist who founded the activist think tank and the Urban Studies Department at Queens, devised a program with admissions criteria requiring that students demonstrate a commitment to social change.

I also had experience with three doctoral programs whose mission was to develop dissertations with emphasis on social change. I received my doctorate from Union Graduate School, an accredited alternative PhD program, which emphasized creating social change. I taught for twenty-five years in Old Dominion University's PhD program in Urban Services, which was designed to produce action research for change in the urban community. Upon retiring, I joined, part time, the faculty of Walden University, an accredited online university, where the idea of social change was paramount for doctoral work. As an adjunct at Old Dominion University, I also taught a class on leadership and social change.

Given this background, one might reasonably assume that my teaching tilted toward encouraging students to hold a certain point of view. Far from it—I taught multiple points of view in a Socratic method.

LEADERSHIP FOR SOCIAL JUSTICE (LSJ)

By the 1900s, a small group of professors—four to be exact—that was fueled by "moral outrage at the unmet needs of students" formed a "grassroots effort" to

> reorient policy and practice in educational administration that was deemed overly focused on technical aspects of educational management at the expense of the moral, social-justice objective of preparing students for equitable participation in democratic society.[6]

The group grew to 150 scholar-practitioners known as the Leadership for Social Justice (LSJ). They wrote a book, *Leadership for Social Justice: Making Revolutions in Education,* in the hopes of presenting a "social justice framework for educational leadership, both theoretically and practically."[7]

The founders of this social justice movement proclaim an "activist, interventionist stance of social justice leadership [that is] inspired not just by an intellectual ideal, but also by moral outrage at the unmet needs of students."[8] The contributors to the book proclaim that the definition of social justice is "linked closely with perspectives on leadership" embodying the "concept of moral transformative leadership."[9] Again, we are told in another essay that "critical interrogation is a moral endeavor that is linked with social justice."[10] They cite Miami University of Ohio's Educational Leadership Program as a prime example of a curriculum that has its "focus on school leadership as an intellectual, moral, and craft practice."[11]

JAMES MACGREGOR BURNS AND TRANSFORMATIVE LEADERSHIP

The father of leadership studies, the political scientist James Macgregor Burns, threw down the gauntlet in 1978 with the publication of his classic work *Leadership.* In that book, Burns announced that transformative leadership must have a moral core in addition to a vision and followers. That template heavily influenced other scholars of leadership who followed in his footsteps. Moreover, he implied an assumption that moral leadership led to social justice.

> In his 2003 follow-up book, *Transforming Leadership,* Burns argued that if leadership is, as I believe, a moral undertaking, a response to the human wants expressed in public values, then surely its greatest task . . . must be to respond to the billions of the world's people in direst want.[12]

Burns joined the Jepson School for Leadership at the University of Richmond in Virginia in 2003, when he was eighty-five, to assemble an interdisciplinary team "to define what a leadership program should encompass." By then, there had developed some nine hundred leadership programs at colleges and universities.[13]

The Jepson School organized its curriculum around a host of courses aimed at developing leadership potential. Among these courses are "Justice and Civil Society," which focuses on an "analysis of poverty and related socio-economic problems," "Leadership in Social Movements," which explores the "values of leaders," and "Ethics and Leadership," which encompasses study of "how moral values and assumptions shape concepts and practices of leadership, including the role of values in determining moral obligations of leaders."[14]

OTHER RELEVANT COURSES

Both the urban studies programs and the black studies programs of the 1960s offered courses where social change was assumed. Indeed, my colleague and mentor at Queens College in New York City, Marilyn Gittell, created an urban studies program at the master of arts level that was primarily designed for students who had been or who were change agents.

By the 1980s the urban and black studies programs were in decline. But their prominence in the liberal arts curriculum was replaced by other equally socially conscious programs, such as women's studies and cultural studies courses. These programs were the direct descendents of the urban and black studies movement. One feminist scholar observed that "blacks insisted on courses that looked at the African-American experience; women demanded courses on the female experience."[15]

The cultural studies phenomenon consisted of courses that one critic described as an "amalgam of sociology, social history, and literature, rewritten as it was a language of contemporary culture."[16] Begun in England in the 1950s, cultural studies blends a neo-Marxist approach with queer theory to become a "politics of difference."

A cultural study was one of the more ambitious curricula developments geared toward social change. A cultural study was intended to broaden a traditional Marxist critique of culture to include race and gender in addition to class as powerful cultural variables.

How well has that experiment succeeded on American campuses? Although many universities have offered cultural studies as a program—but not as permanent departments—the results are mixed. According to the literary critic Michael Bèrubè, writing in the *Chronicle of Higher Education*, "since its importation to the United States, however, cultural studies has basically turned into a branch of pop-culture criticism."[17]

Bèrubè asks rhetorically, "has cultural studies made the American university a more egalitarian or progressive institution?"[18] His answer is that "cultural studies haven't had much of an impact at all."[19] The problem, according to Bèrubè, is that cultural studies has been made "coextensive with the study of popular culture . . . so that . . . it has been effectively conflated with 'cultural criticism,' in general, and associated with a cheery 'Pop culture is fun' approach."[20] Bèrubè quotes Stuart Hall, a British founder of cultural studies, to demonstrate his point: "I really cannot read another cultural-study analysis of Madonna or the *Sopranos*."[21]

Bèrubè concludes his essay with the pessimistic assessment that "cultural studies have had negligible impact on the American academic left in a political sense."[22] Nevertheless, he still hopes "that the history of cultural studies might matter to the university—and to the work beyond it."[23]

JOHN DEWEY AND THE SOCIAL RECONSTRUCTIONISTS

One crucial concept in John Dewey's philosophy of education was the "social spirit." Dewey argued that the school was the social engine that would transform American society. Dewey was one of a group of progressive educators at the beginning of the twentieth century who argued for the social reconstruction of a capitalist America; hence, these progressive educators were called "social reconstructionists."

Dewey argued that "the measure of the worth of the administration, curriculum, and methods of instruction of the school is the extent to which they are animated by the social spirit."[24] Moreover, Dewey equated that social spirit with a moral dimension. "The moral and the social quality of conduct are, in the last analysis," he contends, "equal with each other."[25]

His fellow progressive educator and social reconstructionist George C. Counts went one step further than Dewey. Counts challenged the progressive education movement to enlist the school to actively change society. In a famed address to the Progressive Education Association in 1932 entitled "Dare the Schools Build a New Social Order?" Counts argued that educators should be in the forefront in the "general reconstruction of society through the school."[26]

THE CRITICAL THEORISTS

A group of prominent academics, called the critical theorists, emerged in the mid-1970s, inheriting the tradition of advocating for social reconstruction established by Dewey and Counts. Influenced by these elder scholars, the critical theorists added a blend of neo-Marxism to their studies, emphasizing disparities in race, gender, and class. Among this group were Henry Giroux, Stanley Aronowitz, Michael Apple, and Peter McClaren. Their work brought them academic acclaim and in some cases prestigious endowed professorships. One academic observed that "the radical critique has become increasingly well-known within the mainstream, as indicated by its influence in professional research associations such as AERA [American Educational Research Association]."[27]

One mainstream scholar, Eliot Eisner of Stanford, observed that the critical theorists concentrated on "the social text" from a position that was "almost always on the political left" and that their analyses were "critical—in the negative sense."[28] Nevertheless, Eisner concluded that "critical theory provides one of the most visible and articulate analyses of education found in educational journals and books devoted to the state of schools."[29]

One can readily find exemplary examples of universities striving to change the social paradigm. Among these are Trinity College and Notre Dame.

CASE STUDY: TRINITY COLLEGE

A growing problem with urban universities has been the gradual expansion of poor communities surrounding these colleges and universities as middle-class residents—both black and white—move to the suburbs. In the late 1990s, the president of Trinity College in Hartford, Connecticut, sought to provide a different paradigm to town and gown relations. Rather than relocating the undesirable poor adjacent to the college, Evan S. Dobelle established a vision for university expansion that would *restore* the surrounding neighborhood to Trinity.

This involved buying homes, renovating them, and selling them back to the residents at cut-rate prices. Moreover, these same residents would be mentored and offered opportunities to work at the college. And for the benefit of these residents, three schools—from elementary to high school—would be built. Dobelle was able to raise $175 million from city, state, and federal agencies for his "grand vision." This model paradigm stands alone for its compassion and imagination.[30]

CASE STUDY: NOTRE DAME AND SOCIAL ACTION

The University of Notre Dame, a Catholic university, has created a bevy of social action programs for students, which make it a model university in that regard. When Reverend Theodore Hesburgh—for two decades a prominent member of the U.S. Commission on Civil Rights—entered Notre Dame in 1934, "there was only one student . . . engaged in voluntary public service: bringing food to the poor."[31] Currently, 80 percent of Notre Dame undergraduate students are engaged in a wide variety of voluntary services. And most important, a Notre Dame longitudinal study of lifelong effects of college social involvement indicates that "service-learning appears to be associated with positive long-term impacts."[32]

A large part of the credit for that success goes to Notre Dame's Center for Social Concerns, which was founded in 1983 to coordinate voluntary public service for undergraduates. The Center's philosophical assumptions blend a "2,000 year old moral tradition" steeped in Catholic faith with that of "Dewey's insight that learning is a process of constantly making meaning of the world and one's experience within social contexts."[33] The Center offers academic credit for both domestic and international service programs.

There are summer learning programs with direct student involvement in many aspects of social justice. The international summer placement in eleven countries in 2006 was offered in such diversified programs as orphanages, medical clinics, and health seminars. This program was initiated in 1998. The domestic service-learning program was offered in forty states and offered aid to the poor. In addition, one-credit courses are offered for seminars in communities in Appalachia, in Montreal working with developmentally challenged persons, and in New Orleans working with Hurricane Katrina victims.

In 1998, an eleven-year longitudinal study of the lasting effects of service-learning programs was conducted by three Notre Dame scholars. A sample of 1987's Summer Learning Project students was compared to a sample of students who did not participate in the Summer Learning Project eight-week program. Each group numbered nineteen subjects. The SSP students were placed in medical clinics, homeless shelters, youth centers, and the like. The cohort group had "some service activities as undergraduates" but did not participate in the SSP.[34]

Four variables were measured among the two groups: (1) "commitment to a life of service"; (2) "relationship to society"; (3) "spirituality"; and (4) "growth."[35] The authors of the study concluded that "previous service-learning (SSP) participants scored higher than those in the comparison group on all four dependent variables."[36]

THE COMMUNITY
OF SCHOLARS

What are the aims of education? Harvard philosopher Alfred North Whitehead offers a classic, thoroughly American answer in his 1929 essay, "The Aims of Education":

> What education has to impart is an intimate sense for the power of ideas, for the beauty of ideas, and for the structure of ideas, together with a particular body of knowledge which has peculiar reference to the life of the being possessing it.[1]

But the aims of education vary with the constituency. According to Derek Bok in *Our Underachieving Colleges*, faculty agrees "almost unanimously that teaching students to think critically is the principal aim of undergraduate education."[2] Critical thinking is devolution of Dewey's definition of thinking and learning as solving *real* problems. The general public, according to a *New York Times* article, considers a "traditional liberal arts education" as emphasizing "critical thinking, civic and historical knowledge and ethical reasoning."[3] Although some students seek intellectual growth, many are intent on preparing for a career.

FACULTY

The faculty is the key component to university life. The relationship of professors to their students, to the advancement of knowledge, and to their professional community determines the quality of the college experience; indeed, faculty is judged by their peers in terms of that triad: teaching, research, and service. Moreover, as college presidents speak less on national and global matters, faculty members become moral leaders as they assume roles as public intellectuals.

The first responsibility of faculty is to teach—the first component of the triad. Recent attacks on universities center on the alleged lack of teaching, which allows the faculty to pursue research. According to Derek Bok in *Our Underachieving Colleges*, "the most frequent complaint is that professors are so preoccupied with research and consulting that they neglect their teaching and ignore students."[4] Bok claims that "the charge turns out to be simplistic."[5]

Bok refutes the criticism by citing a U.S. Department of Education study that shows that faculty members devote more than half their time on teaching and less than 20 percent on research. Indeed. Less than half of the faculty publishes one academic refereed article per year.[6] Few consult. And more than three-fourths of students indicate that they are satisfied with their professors.[7]

Still, the attack on universities is relentless. Matthew Miller, a syndicated columnist, characterizes the "dubious research" of faculty as "idle, tenure-earning junk with little or no social value."[8] He advocates eliminating "100,000 of today's 550,000 full-time professors without students noticing," since 20 percent of professors spend time doing research.[9]

Rather than a process of promoting "idle junk," the research process is rigorous in the field of education. Completed research must pass peer review for publication in both academic journals and scholarly books. Moreover, research findings presented at academic conferences are subject to peer review. Approximately 95 percent of articles sent to academic journals in education are rejected for questionable methodology and educational insignificance. The same is true for scholarly monographs.

Defenders of the necessity for research often point to the connection between research and teaching. Janet Lyon, a professor at Penn State, recipient of a university teaching award, and the author of *Manifestoes*, "absolutely believes that research is essential to keep professors on the cutting edge of knowledge so as to increase their teaching effectiveness."[10] In this respect she echoes the sentiments of Stanley Aronowitz, who feels that "the more original research, the better," so that professors do not "become stale after a decade of teaching, regardless of their age."[11]

Jeffrey Glanz argues that "research keeps one alive and on the cutting edge of latest research."[12] He cautions, however, that "one who is involved in research is not necessarily an effective teacher or a more effective one than one who doesn't regularly conduct research."[13] That said, he contends that "research keeps one's energies and motivations flowing, which can have a positive carryover to teaching."[14]

James Koch follows up Glanz's points, saying that he has "known some very good teachers who weren't researchers; they had active minds and were voracious readers" but "they are the exceptions."[15] Still, Koch believes "that teaching and research are connected" and that "it's very difficult for someone to remain current in their teaching if they are not doing research."[16] Moreover, he argues "some of the best research ideas come from classrooms when students ask questions."[17]

Diane Ravitch demurs from the argument that research makes for a better teacher. "Not necessarily," she claims, since she feels that "much research is tendentious"; For Ravitch, an effective teacher "should be aware of debates, issues, conflicts."[18]

CANON REVISION

What should a professor teach? In the past generation, a culture war erupted over the question of curriculum. Modernists maintained a steady advocacy for a "great books" curriculum, which often meant works by white male Americans and Europeans—the Western canon. For example, Anthony T. Kronman in his book *Education's End* (2007) presents a dated list in his course in the humanities at Yale. In the fall of 2005, his literary classics end with Dante; his spring 2006 list of great books ends with T. S. Eliot.[19]

A generation of young postmodern faculty argued the need to update curricula for fresh perspectives. They emphasized the dynamics of race, gender, class, and a global perspective. In educational foundations courses, one would be constrained by a curriculum that ended with Dewey. Surely, the question of IQ and standardized testing needs to confront Howard Gardner's theory of multiple intelligences (*Frames of Mind*, 1983). And in educational psychology, one must take into account Carol Gilligan's research on the moral development of women (*In a Different Voice*, 1982). In short, the canon needs constant revision.

For some, the culture wars have ended. For others, they still linger. Diane Ravitch emphatically states that the culture wars "are dead" since "everyone got tired and bored and stopped caring."[20] Moreover, she argues that "one side got exhausted and crept away."[21] Michael Bèrubè feels that "the culture wars will go on as long as you have wing nuts out there" who seek to "get the liberals off campuses."[22] He asks, "why are people still hating Toni Morrison?"[23] He answers his own question with the contention that "in the Canon-Debating World, it is always 1987."[24]

And still others take the long view. Dana Heller, director of the humanities program at Old Dominion University and author of *The Selling of 9/11* (2005), finds the recent culture wars as mainly a "journalistic label" and contends "American culture has always been a metaphorical battlefield."[25] She believes that "culture must be fought over" and "if it appears that the culture wars have died it's not because the humanities have given up the work" but because "the mass media has turned its attention to a different set of very immediate conflicts, probably without recognizing that these, too, are cultural."[26]

FACULTY AS MORAL LEADERS

In recent years, university presidents of both public and private institutions have felt constrained about speaking out on local, national, and international issues that could alienate funding constituencies. A 1994 study of university presidents on this matter concluded that "college and university presidents are perceived as silent and lacking in leadership on important public policy issues."[27] The author, Rita Bornstein, president of Rollins College, discovered that presidents fear "offending diverse constituencies" when speaking out on controversial issues because of a possible negative "impact on fundraising."[28]

Consequently, the role of moral leader in the community has fallen on professors, albeit by default. A handful of college professors at various universities serve as the academic conscience of America. Given the sobriquet of "public intellectuals," these professors write for newspapers and intellectual magazines and appear on television and radio, sharing their expertise on contemporary issues.

Unfortunately, academic public intellectuals often pay a price for their leadership. Writing for the public media does not count in academic determinations for tenure or promotion. Colleagues often view the work of public intellectuals as nonacademic. Yet public intellectuals often base their observations on contemporary issues on the research they have conducted as scholars. Moreover, university administrators are often skittish about the provocative comments made by public intellectual professors. Government officials who are criticized in the press often complain to university presidents, creating a chilling effect on campus.

STUDENTS

On April 16, 2007, a mentally unbalanced student at Virginia Tech horrified the world by killing thirty-two students and faculty. Seun Hui Cho fell through the cracks of the mental health system in school and college. The incident was a turning point in safety protection across campuses in the United States.

Governor Tim Kaine of Virginia appointed a review panel to assess what went wrong. The panel interviewed more than two hundred people and examined thousands of pages of records. The panel established a history of mental illness beginning with Cho's childhood. It also concluded that the university had failed to "intervene effectively," despite clear signs of Cho's instability known to various professors and departments.[29] In the panel's words, "no one connected the dots."[30]

Complicating easy access to records of Cho's illness were federal and Virginia privacy laws that hindered knowledge of the seriousness of Cho's condition. Virginia is one of twenty-two states that report data to a federal database about the mental health background of prospective gun purchasers. However, since Cho was an outpatient and not committed to an institution, he was allowed to buy a gun.

Another problem in the case was the campus police "prematurely concluding" that after the first shooting, the "'person of interest' probably was no longer on campus."[31] Moreover, the campus police erred in not requesting "a campus warning" that "students and staff should be cautious and alert."[32]

The question of campus violence is paramount to a university administration that is entrusted with responsibility—in loco parentis—for the welfare of students. One study estimated that nearly half a million acts of violence are committed against college students yearly.[33] These acts include homicide, sexual assault and sexual harassment, stalking, rape, and racial and ethnic violence. The impact of these acts on victims is psychological and physiological. Victims of sexual harassment, for example, change careers, drop out of classes, and suffer loss of morale and lost confidence in their studies.[34]

Students are required to behave morally in their academic life. Nevertheless, a large majority of students admit to cheating at college, and the problem is getting worse.[35] In addition to cheating on tests, students often plagiarize their term papers. It is convenient for students to purchase a term paper on the Internet, and it is difficult for professors to determine who wrote the paper. Colleges and universities have adopted honor codes to monitor cheating, but enforcement is lax, and studies show that few professors report cheating to the proper authorities. This situation has prompted Derek Bok to conclude that "instruction in ethics is needed all the more today."[36]

THE ADMINISTRATION

University administrations have had a notable long and steadfast history of preserving affirmative action in hiring professors and admitting students. They have sought to incorporate what Amy Gutmann, president of the University of Pennsylvania and co-author of *Color Conscious* (1996) subtitled "the political morality of race." In addition, universities have been sensitive, for the most part, to gender issues.

Affirmative action was the embodiment of the concept of "equality of results" proclaimed by President Lyndon Johnson in his speech "To Fulfill These Rights" at Howard University in 1965.

There is ample evidence that affirmative action programs at universities succeed in aiding black students to rise socially and economically. A 1998 study, *The Shape of the River*, by William G. Bowen, president of Princeton University, and Derek Bok, president of Harvard, dramatically showed the benefits of affirmative action. Bowen and Bok took a sample of elite universities and colleges and followed students in 1976 and 1989.

Overwhelmingly, black and Hispanic students from these classes graduated from college, medical, and law schools.[37]

Two questions confront policies of affirmative action. Are these policies to be continued in perpetuity? The concept of equality of results clashes with the doctrine of fairness to all stakeholders enunciated by John Rawls in his classic philosophical treatise *A Theory of Justice* (1971). For Rawls, social justice depends on each participant receiving a measure of satisfaction. Nevertheless, Rawls made an exception to his theory for race, suggesting that affirmative action programs—although unfair to some groups—be pursued at least for fifty years, which was the model of social mobility of European ethnics in the twentieth century. It has been almost fifty years since Johnson declared a policy of "equality of results," and the prospects of affirmative action programs fading in universities is rather dim, despite occasional movements to dismantle these programs. And the other question is whether the "political morality of race," as Gutmann calls it, should be modified to include class as well. Gutmann observes that university admissions constitute "the realm in which class should supplant race as a qualification" to enable poor deserving students an educational opportunity to enter the middle class.[38] But Gutmann, a political philosopher, rejects the idea of "class not race" in favor of one of a "color conscious" university that maintains the educational policy of affirmative action for African Americans.[39]

GENDER BIAS
IN ACADEMIA

Although universities pursue affirmative action policies that favor African Americans and women, they are often guilty of gender bias. This takes place in tenure, promotion, and salary among faculty members and the teachers of women students in the sciences. On the plus side, universities have had to follow the dictates of the Title IX federal mandate to provide athletic programs for girls. But that venture is still problematic—despite the gains—due to the lack of policing of the programs by federal authorities.

One reason for gender bias is the unconscious teaching by instructors to the boys. These teachers are not aware that they favor the boys in discussions in class. This phenomenon is characteristic of teachers in schools from kindergarten to graduate school. In their classic tome, *Failing at Fairness: How Our Schools Cheat Girls* (1994), Myra and David Sadker reported this phenomenon:

> The students most likely to receive teacher attention were white males; the second most likely were minority males; the third, white females; and the least likely, minority females.[1]

At universities, the Sadkers discovered that "men receive 75 percent of the doctoral degrees in business and 91 percent in engineering" while women comprise the "soft sciences," such as education.[2]

Gender bias infects even the highest levels at top universities. In 2005, the president of Harvard University, Lawrence H. Summers, attributed the lack of females in science and math not to classroom discrimination but to the innate genetic differences between men and women.[3]

TENURE PROMOTION AND SALARY

In 2009, Anne M. Schoening pointed out in an article in the *Journal of Women in Educational Leadership* that "more than half of all research doctorates granted to U.S. citizens are awarded to women" yet "women comprise only 34 percent of full-time faculty in doctoral institutions."[4] She claims that women are "shying away from careers in higher education" because of "the demands of motherhood, coupled with a lack of family friendly policies in the academic workplace."[5]

Schoening contends that the present tenure system "is an antiquated practice based on the traditional career paths and life events of men."[6] Since the average age of women with newly minted doctorates is thirty-four, this coincides "with women's childbearing age."[7] And women who seek tenure are "21 percent less likely to achieve it than men."[8] She also notes that the reasons women fail to achieve tenure "may be unrelated to marriage and family."[9] She contents that "23 percent of the gender salary gap in academia is due to discrimination."[10] She writes that

> Disparities in rank, tenure status, and pay are deeply ingrained in the American academic culture and have been slow to change, particularly at the most competitive and prestigious schools.[11]

Shoening endorses the recommendations of the American Associate of University Professors (AAUP) regarding strategies to increase the number of tenured female faculty. The AAUP advises that "institutions should adopt tenure policies that do not create conflicts between having children and establishing optimal research records."[12] In that respect, the AAUP suggests that universities stop the tenure clock "for one or two years for birth or adoption of children."[13]

Another recent study published in 2009 by the University of California Berkeley's Mary Ann Mason points out that "too many" potential female scholars decide not to pursue careers in science, technology, engineering, and mathematics (STEM) fields "because of interest in starting a family."[14] The authors of the four-year study found that at sixty-two "pre-eminent research universities that receive the bulk of federal science money" that "43 percent received no leave policies for graduate-student mothers."[15]

TITLE IX

Passed in 1972, the federal law Title IX covers all aspects of education; the effect for girls and women is "more opportunities than any previous generation."[16] Dramatic increases in college attendance for females resulted, in part, from Title IX. But for most people, Title IX has involved progress in sports. Nevertheless, complaints have arisen that Title IX needs enforcing.

In 1972, girls did not play Little League; today some 360,000 girls play. In 1972, 300,000 high school girls and fewer than 30,000 women were involved in athletics, compared to the three million high school girls and 155,000 college women playing sports today.[17] Nevertheless, increased spending on men's football and basketball teams has diminished the amount allocated to college women's sports.

A 2009 report by the National Women's Law Center charges that the U.S. Education Department's Office of Civil Rights "has cut back sharply in the number of athletic programs it evaluates," resulting in the inability to sufficiently enforce "gender equity in college sports."[18] The report concludes that "more women than ever are participating in college sports" but "poor treatment of women persists."[19]

President Barack Obama promised on the campaign trail that he would seek enforcement of Title IX, specifically for athletic programs. "Compliance review has dropped," he declared, "the focus of reviews has narrowed, and the agency has taken a lax approach to enforcement."[20]

Moreover, in the month before his election, President Obama promised to significantly increase the number of women in science and technology. He told the members of the Association for Women in Science and the Society of Women Engineers that he would do more to enforce Title IX, which prevents discrimination in educational programs. And his secretary of education, Arne Duncan, issued a statement on the thirty-seventh anniversary of Title IX that the law was crucial in encouraging women "to pursue their aspirations in fields in which they have been historically underrepresented, such as science and technology."[21]

WOMEN AND SCIENCE

Perhaps the most symbolic event highlighting gender bias in higher education occurred in January 14, 2005, when the president of Harvard University, Lawrence H. Summers, declared that women were not as successful as men in science and math careers due to innate genetic differences. Moreover, his remarks were made at a conference at Harvard for the National Bureau of Economic Research on women and minorities in science and engineering. A number of attendees were offended by Summers's statements.

The uproar over Summers's remarks went beyond the confines of Harvard's campus to the national media. The president of the National Organization for Women, Kim Gandy, issued a press release condemning the remarks:

Summers' suggestion that women are inferior to men in their ability to excel at math and science is more than an example of personal sexism, it is a clue to why women have not been more fully accepted and integrated into the tenured faculty at Harvard since he has been president.[22]

During his tenure at Harvard, the number of female tenured faculty declined—only four of the last thirty-two tenure offers were made to women in the faculty of arts and sciences.[23] The controversy resulted in Summers's resignation and the hiring of Harvard's first female president, Drew Gilpin Faust.

The landscape is changing dramatically for women in science and engineering. In 2005, women earned as many doctorates as men for the first time ever; one fourth were in the physical sciences and 18 percent were in engineering.[24] And in 2009, three U.S. women were awarded the Nobel Prize in science.

The underrepresentation of women in science and engineering fields has been well documented and continues to be a theme in current research. In spite of gains, gaps still exist between women and men in terms of their college-level enrollment in science, mathematics, and engineering. Kerry K. Karukstis points out in an essay in the *Chronicle of Higher Education* that one problem with the current research is that studies on gender disparity in those fields are mostly targeted at the top research universities. Often overlooked are "universities with less-extensive levels of research support."[25]

And according to Ajda Kahueci, Sherry A. Southerland, and Penny J. Gilmer in *The Journal of Science Teaching*, efforts to increase students in STEM fields "often target K–12 education" but "are not as visible at the college level."[26] These researchers examined students in their first year of a STEM program at a research university in the American southeast. Thirty-five participants were involved in the research. They lived together in a residence hall. They took a one-credit course, "Women in Science Colloquium," where campus female scientists would describe their research. In addition, the students were involved in lectures, panel discussions, mentoring, tutoring, and field trips. The researchers concluded that "the women support and retention program at the center of the study was successful in retaining students in their intended STEM majors."[27]

There have been support groups cropping up in recent years to offer support to women who enter the hard sciences at the college and university level. One such group is the Association for Women in Science (AWIS). According to their Web site, "The Association for Women in Science is dedicated to achieving equality and full participation for women in science, technology, engineering and mathematics."[28]

The group offers membership, online communities, forums, and networking, mentoring, and funding opportunities, among others. Groups like this are vital lifelines to women struggling to navigate a male-dominated terrain.

One of the ways to expose women to STEM careers is to start early, while they are girls in elementary school. Since many girls have decided against STEM career goals by middle school, it is important to catch them early. Much of this responsibility lies with the classroom teacher. And the classroom teachers' attitudes toward STEM in turn lie in part with the college professor charged with teacher education. At the college and university level, teacher education professors have a large stake in releasing into the workforce new teachers who have their radar trained on girls and science. There have been many efforts in recent years to recruit girls and minorities into STEM tracks, which result in programs aimed at pre-service teachers still enrolled in general education courses at the university level. One such program is described below.

Clair Berube took part in an intensive two-week summer STEM institute for pre-service teachers that took place during in 2009 at NASA Langley, Hampton, Virginia. The focus of the NASA STEM Pre-Service Teacher Program was to teach prospective elementary and middle school teachers who are currently college juniors and seniors or first-year graduate students with no undergraduate degree in education how to develop and teach in an integrated, standards-based STEM curriculum using NASA materials and resources. As the culminating event, the students must teach their newly developed lesson, over a two-day period, to children from a local elementary school, which had students attending during the summer.

The NASA program's students are chosen from more than 150 universities throughout the United States by a competitive process based on their grade-point averages. Twenty-two students were chosen from a large pool from all over the country. The group was ethnically diverse and included African Americans, Caucasians, and Latinos. Most were female. During the two-week institute, the students followed a rigorous schedule, which included lectures and hands-on lessons from science education professors, NASA engineers, and scientists. The students were introduced to STEM concepts, took tours of the NASA facilities, and participated in hands-on labs, activities, and problem solving. Lesson topics included gravity and the moon, flight principles, STEM standards and lessons, shuttle flight mission work, how astronauts solve problems in space, kite flying, and quantum physics. In teams of five and with the guidance of the science education professors, the students used these topics to create STEM lesson plans to teach to elementary students in the local school during a two-day period at the end of the institute. The lessons taught to the children included an egg-drop activity and principles of flight activity. The NASA students were also fortunate enough to meet Dr. Charles Bolden, the newly appointed director of NASA, who was visiting Langley on his tour of facilities.

Each day ended with a debriefing by the students, faculty, and administrators of the institute to discuss the day's work and to plan for the next day. Students came away with a renewed excitement and love for science and with a charge to recruit more girls and minorities into science careers when they enter their own classrooms as teachers. This effort must begin early and must be maintained throughout middle and high school, because although girls may be naturally gifted in STEM areas, they become discouraged by the lack of support by the time they reach middle school. Programs such as this one offer hope and encouragement to girls and minorities who show interest and ability in STEM subjects.

There is a riddle that I (Clair) offer to my university students when I begin my lecture on gender and science: A man and his son are in a terrible car accident. The man is killed instantly and the son is rushed to the emergency room. The surgeon arrives, looks at the boy, and says, "I can't operate on this boy, because he is my son!" How is this possible if the father was killed in the accident? After a moment, students begin their guesses: "Was the surgeon the boy's stepfather?" Although many of my students profess to be feminists, most do not get this riddle. I have been offering this riddle in classes during the last ten years, and most still do not get it. The answer, of course, is that the surgeon is the boy's mother. When the students hear this answer, their faces show instant understanding of how they can unconsciously perpetuate the bias while unaware of it. We think that gender bias is a conscious act perpetrated by bigots and misogynists who only want to keep women in the kitchen. But it is kept alive by people who are for women's equality and rights but who have unconscious beliefs about what women can and cannot do. This belief is under the radar of our conscious thought and a remnant of an era when women had very few choices. Although we have come a long way, there is a cultural lag between what we intellectually know to be true and what we still believe and feel. This is yet to be overcome.

THE UNIVERSITY
AND THE NATION

What is the moral relationship between the university and the nation? If we assume, as does critical theorist Henry Giroux, that "higher education is a moral and political enterprise," should the university be servant to a warfare state?[1] Or to industry?

Clark Kerr in his classic jeremiad, *The Uses of the University*, contends that "the university has become a prime instrument of national purpose "signaling a 'transformation'" that was "new" to higher education.[2] Or should the university organize against a military-industrial-academic complex as Giroux suggests in his 2007 book *The University in Chains: Confronting the Military-Industrial-Academic Complex*?

Kerr's definition of "national purpose" left much to be desired. It was an ambiguous phrase that implied that the university should endorse any national policy pursued by the federal government. Indeed, most academicians have supported the close collaboration of university and industry and the military. Opposing them since World War II is a small group of liberals and radicals who perceive danger to democracy and to the university by blindly supporting the government's pursuit of military and industrial strength in foreign policy.

No less a person than President Dwight D. Eisenhower warned in his famous farewell speech in 1961 of a "military-industrial complex."[3] Eisenhower had originally intended to include "academic" in that phrase but deleted it on second thought. It was left to Senator William Fulbright, an outspoken opponent of the Vietnam War, to rephrase it to "military-industrial-academic complex" later in the decade.[4] Speaking of the "military-industrial-complex," Eisenhower presciently warned that "we must never let the weight of this combination endanger our liberties or democratic process."[5] Fulbright criticized that a "university fails its higher purpose" by "lending itself too much to the purposes of government."[6]

THE UNIVERSITY AND THE MILITARY

The relationship between universities and the defense industry began with the Cold War in 1950. At that time, 87 percent of federal funding for academic research was commissioned by the Pentagon and the Atomic Energy Commission.[7] In 1952, 96 percent of federal funding for social sciences came from the military.[8]

According to Stuart W. Leslie in his book *The Cold War and American Science: The Military-Industrial-Academic Complex at MIT and Stanford*, "the Cold War redefined American science."[9] The Department of Defense accounted for 80 percent of federal research money—$5.5 billion by 1960. "The Korean War completed the mobilization of American science," Leslie writes, "and made the university, for the first time, a full partner in the military-industrial complex."[10] The phrase "big sciences" was introduced to describe how "the military set the paradigm for postwar American science."[11] Leslie concludes that "without question, the university showed what it could do in the name of national defense, but at what cost to itself and, ultimately, the nation?"[12]

Leslie rivetingly portrays Cold War science at two elite universities: Massachusetts Institute of Technology (MIT) and Stanford. Both universities placed high on the list of defense research funding from the Department of Defense (DOD) and Atomic Energy Commission. In 1968, MIT received $119 million for research from the DOD.[13] Stanford received $50 million from the Atomic Energy Commission in the 1960s.[14]

But the 1960s brought a controversial war—Vietnam—which had a universal draft that impacted college students as well as the general populace. Students and faculty reacted against the "war research" at a number of elite schools. In 1969, the MIT faculty held a strike of sorts for a "day of reflection" on the "abuses of science."[15] The MIT faculty were alarmed at "the militarization of American science."[16] Moreover, the radical student organization Students for a Democratic Society later protested the recruitment of students from Dow Chemical, which produced the deadly napalm used by American forces in Vietnam.[17] In 1966, students and faculty picketed administrative offices at Stanford over covert CIA contracts.[18] Columbia saw students demonstrate against the university's Institute for Defense Analysis, and Harvard students resisted the establishment of the Reserve Officers Training Corps (ROTC) on campus.[19]

By the 1960s, the relationship between the academy and industry and defense was solidified. Two-thirds of academic research still went to the DOD, the Atomic Energy Commission, or the National Aeronautics and Space Administration.[20] Ten elite universities received 38 percent of these funds, including Harvard, Columbia, MIT, Stanford, and Chicago.[21] This prompted journalist James Ridgeway to write in a 1968 expose, *The Closed Corporation: American Universities in Crisis*, a searing indictment of how universities have "sold out to industry and the war machine."[22]

The post–9/11 world saw a renewed national purpose directed toward fighting terrorism. Critical of universities' "new collaboration between the national security state and higher education,"

Henry Giroux notes the "resurgence of patriotic commitment and uncritical support" of the academy toward "increasing militarization."[23] Giroux quotes a 2002 report by the Association of American Universities that 60 percent of defense research is allocated to some 350 universities.[24] Giroux charges that

> Military research on campuses has dangerous implications for the academy and for the social order. It produces lethal weapons, subverts the peaceful use of scientific knowledge, fuels an arms race, debases the talents of faculty and students, promotes secrecy and prevents full disclosure, and *corrupts the ethical standards of the university.*[25]

Giroux advocates a strategy to confront the military-industrial-academic complex by having faculty engage as "public intellectuals" who turn "the university into a vibrant critical site of learning and an unconditional site of pedagogical political resistance."[26] Moreover, he adds that this resistance "means stepping out of the classroom and working with others" to redirect the priorities of the university.[27]

THE UNIVERSITY AND INDUSTRY

The collaboration of universities and industry was chronicled in a 2005 book, *University, Inc.: The Corporate Corruption of American Higher Education,* by Jennifer Washburn. Washburn writes that since 1980 "a foul wind has blown over the campuses of our nation's universities [which is] the growing role those commercial values have assumed in academic life."[28] This development, she argues, began in the 1970s "in response to heightened competition from Japan and other countries," so that American universities were urged "to forge closer ties with private industry, convert themselves into engines of economic growth, and pump out commercially valuable invention."[29] Consequently, she believes that "the single greatest threat to the future of American higher education [is] the intrusion of a market ideology into the heart of academic life."[30]

Washburn argues that industry replaced the federal "golden age" of military funding by the 1970s. She cites examples of industry invading the scientific research departments of universities. For example, in 1974 Harvard Medical School accepted $23.5 million from Monsanto, an agricultural company, to do cancer research. In 1983, Columbia struck a deal with Bristol-Myers.[31] And Washburn offers the example Berkeley, which took $25 million from a Swiss pharmaceutical company, Novartis, to fund research. In exchange for the money, Berkeley granted the company one-third rights to research discoveries. Moreover, Novartis was given two of the five seats on the department's research committee. The collaboration resulted in a protest from graduate students who formed a group, Students for Responsible Research, that challenged the relationship between Berkeley and Novartis as being in "conflict with our mission as a university."[32]

Still, Washburn does not believe that "it is realistic to demand that these institutions simply wall themselves off from private industry."[33] She contends that "universities can make vital contributions to scientific and technological innovation and collaborate with industry."[34] But she argues that changes are needed, including "a revamped set of conflict-of-interest regulations, and stronger federal oversight of clinical drug research."[35]

Henry Giroux specifies the incursions of the corporate world onto university campuses. He writes that

> many universities seem less interested in higher learning than in becoming licensed storefronts for brand name corporations—selling office space, buildings, and endowed chairs to rich corporate donors [and] college dining halls [to] McDonalds and Starbucks.
>
> In addition, housing, alumni relations, health care, and a vast array of other services are being leased out to private interests.[36]

He concludes that "there is a new intimacy between higher education and corporate culture."[37]

SOME OPINIONS

Former Old Dominion University president James V. Koch warns of multiple threats to the moral mission of the university:

> Collaboration between universities and the defense establishment could place universities in positions that violate the basic premises upon which the academy operates. . . . But, so also could collaboration with government bodies, businesses, the media, nonprofit institutions, political parties, other universities, etc.
>
> During my fifteen years as a president, on at least one occasion, each of these other organizations attempted to subvert what I view as the basic purposes of the university.[38]

Michael Bèrubè questions why defense is always singled out for criticism. He claims there is a Vietnam syndrome among radical critics, and they are "still fighting Vietnam, and it's all about Dow and napalm."[39] Bèrubè cites Cary Nelson and Steven Watt's book, *Academic Keywords*, for other corruptions of the academy.

Corporate professorships include the Boeing Company Chair in aeronautics at the California Institute of Technology, the Coca-Cola Professors of Marketing at both the University of Arizona and the University of Georgia, the LaQuinta Motor Inns Professor of Business at the University of Texas, the Taco Bell Distinguished Professor of Hotel and Restaurant Administration at Washington State University, the K-Mart Professor of Marketing at Wayne State University, the McLamore/Burger King Chair at the University of Miami, the LEGO Professor of Learning Research and the Chevron Professor of Chemical Engineering at MIT, the Federal Express Chair of Information-Management Systems at the University of Memphis, the General Mills Chair of Cereal Chemistry and Technology at the University of Minnesota, the Coral Petroleum Industries Chair in renewable-energy resources at the University of Hawaii at Manoa, the LaRoche Industries Chair in chemical engineering at the Georgia Institute of Technology, the Ralston-Purina endowed professorship in small-animal nutrition at the university of Missouri at Columbia, the Merck Company Chair in biochemistry and molecular biology at the University of Pennsylvania, the Sears Roebuck Chair in retail marketing at Marquette University, and several corporate-funded chairs at UCLA: the Allstate Chair in finance and insurance, the Nippon Sheet Glass Company Chair in materials science, the Hughes Aircraft Company Chair in manufacturing engineering, and the Rockwell International Chair of Engineering.

As Julianne Basinger reports, MIT has an astonishing sixty-nine corporate-funded chairs, while Stanford so far has but twenty-two. We may add to these about a hundred "free enterprise" chaired professorships across the country, sometimes named after a company, sometimes named after a donor, sometimes named after a conservative business-funded foundation. We have the Gerken Professor of Enterprise and Society at the University of California at Irvine, the Goodyear Professorship of Free Enterprise at Kent State, the Scott L. Probasco Professor of Free Enterprise at Tennessee, and the MasterCard International Distinguished Chair in entrepreneurial leadership at the University of Virginia. The right-wing Olin Foundation has endowed professorships at a dozen universities.[40]

Jeffrey Glanz takes a more moderate stance. He believes that "the Ivory tower paradigm, wherein the university operates in a vacuum, isolated and independent, is antiquated."[41] He writes:

> Universities can no longer remain disconnected, economically, politically, or otherwise from the realities and exigencies of a global world community. . . . The university today must, in fact, interact and take stands on a variety of issues as well as form alliances with constituents and agencies from diverse perspectives.
>
> Universities are thus free to align with the State Department or any other government agency. It is the right and obligation, however, for others within that same university to challenge such alliances.[42]

Peter Steinfels feels that

> The only grounds for a blanket rejection of all cooperation between the university and business and the university and the military as immoral would be that one held a capitalist market economy to be altogether immoral or that one was an absolute pacifist.[43]

Steinfels does not subscribe to "those sweeping positions" he cites; he argues that there "is plenty of room for fierce moral opposition to specific cases of collaboration."[44] Still, he contends that "there may be major good that can be accomplished by collaborative efforts, from medical research to for-profit humanitarian innovation."[45] Moreover, he is "not one to brush aside all national security or foreign policy concerns as inconsequential."[46]

CONCLUSION

The idea of the university has been seriously challenged during the past sixty years. Once, American universities reached out to service the unfortunate. This is still being done with imaginative programs and much dedication of staff. However, the co-optation of universities by the military and business has clouded the nature of the university. And, as Henry Giroux points out, that collaboration shunted aside the universities concentrating on social policy.

The Cold War cast a dark cloud over the development of American universities. In their haste to become legitimate contributors to the national welfare, universities have often strayed from their purpose. They have uncritically supported a foreign policy that was morally questionable at best. Even in his declining years, Clark Kerr regretted the path that universities took beginning in the 1960s.

Does that mean that American universities should refrain from extending their research arm to the needs of national policy? Not necessarily. But the fact remains that American foreign policy since World War II has not been unilaterally supported by the American people in the way that the "good war" was supported. The wars in Vietnam, Grenada, and Iraq were opposed by a segment of the American public—including some students and faculty—as international interventions in pursuit of ideological and economic interests. Indeed, America has conducted its foreign policy based on the Machiavellian principle of realpolitik, where the end justifies the means. What began as a challenge to brutal communist dictatorships devolved into the sanctioning of torture.

Equally pernicious has been the encroachment of the business world onto university campuses. On the plus side, business can better deliver certain campus services, such as dining, than can university staff. However, there can be ethical violations when research is commissioned by industry. Moreover, the selling of the university through endowed professorship and named buildings could possibly compromise the nature of the academy. The humorist Art Buchwald spoofed that collaboration by hypothesizing about Mafia-endorsed projects like the Don Corleone Library.

Nevertheless, critics such as Washburn and Giroux may have missed the mark about a transformation of the university that is more profound in nature. The historian Christopher J. Lucas observed that the very structure of the university has changed so that "the emergence of American higher education as a corporate enterprise" is complete, whereby "much of the trappings of large scale business organization" from mission statements and strategic planning to elaborate budget systems, cost-benefit analysis, and marketing research are put into place.[47]

What can we conclude? The American university is far from finished in its development, and one must be ever vigilant to preserve its educational function free from outside influences that would compromise it.

7

TOWARD A
MORAL UNIVERSITY

The American variant of the university—the service university—is rooted in a profound moral concept and tradition. Unlike its European peers, the American service university continues to address the needs and problems of American society in diverse ways. It has no peers in the Western tradition.

Philip G. Altbach, director of the International Higher Education Center at Boston College and a pioneer in comparative education, considers the American service university "rather unique" and notes that there does not at the moment exist scholarship "that discusses this specific theme."[1] And professor Sophie Body-Gendrot, co-director of the Urban Studies program at the Sorbonne in Paris, observes that in Europe, "it is quite unusual to have joint programs with the university and the city in general."[2] Another close observer of the American education scene, Francesca Gobbo, professor of intercultural studies at the University of Turin, Italy, notes that in Italy "certain types of social initiatives are left to grassroots organizations (either Catholic or leftist) and most of them have no connection with the university."[3]

However, in developing countries in Latin America, Altbach finds that "many Catholic universities have social service activities that they sponsor for students."[4] This is true, he adds, for "lots of Christian and some Hindu colleges in India."[5]

THE UNIVERSITY AND THE COMMUNITY

There was a time when relations between universities and their communities relations were severely strained. Part of that relationship was due to a national policy that encouraged universities to expand into their surrounding neighborhoods and to pursue urban renewal. In 1949, Congress passed Section 112 of the National Housing Act, encouraging universities to pursue urban renewal in their cities by offering a dollar of federal money for every dollar universities spend to revitalize their neighborhoods. Urban renewal was pejoratively called "black removal" by many African American residents in the cities.

The result was conflict between town and gown. A coalition of residents and students and some professors crossed class lines in opposition to the encroachment of their universities. Describing the relationship between his university, Wayne State, and the community, William Deane Smith of the Center for Urban Studies called it a poisoning so that the university "has also acquired a reputation of being the 'enemy' of the local resident."[6] Indeed, a comprehensive study of town-gown relations among 102 urban universities found that between 1952 and 1972, nearly 80 percent of universities surveyed reported "some level of tension with neighbors."[7]

No university was spared conflict resulting from their urban renewal attempts. The list of universities embroiled with their communities includes the University of Chicago, Harvard, Columbia, Berkeley, University of Pittsburgh, Boston College, Temple, Tufts, and the University of Pennsylvania, among others. The University of Chicago can claim the dubious honor of pressuring Congress to pass Section 112.

By the mid-1960s, urban renewal took another direction. Universities, in cooperation with city administrations, were persuaded to invest in low-cost housing in their neighborhoods. Now universities are praised for their community outreach.

Evan S. Dobelle, the former president of Trinity College and engineer of the revitalization of the surrounding neighborhood in New Haven in the 1990s, now issues a report card on the "best neighbor" colleges and universities in the nation. The first survey was released in 2006, the second in 2009.

Dobelle, now president of Westfield State College, and his staff took more than a year to compile data from institutions of higher learning that had "positive economic, social, and cultural impact . . . on the cities in which they reside."[8] The survey "does not include colleges and universities that reside in smaller, more traditional 'college towns.'"[9] The result was that Dobelle and his colleagues identified twenty-five colleges and universities that were "saviors of our cities"; an additional 135 institutions appeared on an "honor roll."[10]

Dobelle states the purpose of the survey as

> not to measure the effectiveness of one institution's efforts versus another's . . . [but to] . . . document, publicize, and advance the unique and innovative means by which concerned and committed colleges and universities forge beneficial and permanent relationships with the communities in which they reside.[11]

The survey is a thirty-two-page document requiring elaborate essay responses that could pass as a self-study for accreditation. The methodology of the survey was both qualitative and quantifiable with the site-visit interviews. Dobelle's schemata included ten criteria including "length of involvement with the community," "real dollars invested," "catalyst effect on others," "presence felt through payroll," and "faculty and student involvement in community service."[12]

The twenty-five universities in the survey include the University of Pennsylvania and the University of Southern California, which tied for first place and "transformed the neighborhood schools" in each case.[13] Other top universities were University of Pittsburgh, whose "neighborhood collaborations have resulted in physically and economically revitalized neighborhoods."[14] The researchers found that St. Louis University, a Catholic university, "reflects the best of the Jesuit devotion to the inner city poor."[15] Those on the honor roll include Brown University, Columbia

University, New York University, Georgetown University, Tufts University, and Yale University, among elite schools.

Parenthetically, in November 2009, Old Dominion University launched a Habitat for Humanity venture that would build a home for a neighborhood family. Faculty, staff, and students formed a building crew in the "hundreds" as "part of a campus-wide community service project."[16] University president John R. Broderick called the effort "an opportunity for ODU to show its volunteer spirit and its commitment to the community."[17]

FACULTY

For faculty, the first moral responsibility in a truly moral university is the transmission of knowledge. This would require faculty to be active research scholars, which puts them on the cutting edge of knowledge.

Faculty would also be conscious of their own inner ideological biases. As Michael Apple and other critical theorists have pointed out, teachers bring to the classroom a "hidden curriculum" of personal values that shape the discussions. And research-based teaching is not value free. Research depends on the questions asked, and these flow from the assumptions of the researcher.

Michael J. Sandel gives us an exemplary case study of how to teach the moral conundrum of affirmative action. Sandel is a leftist who unabashedly argues for affirmative action. There is no hidden curriculum in his teaching. Yet in the companion book to his teaching, *Justice: What's the Right Thing to Do?* Sandel presents the case pro and con in a chapter on arguing affirmative action.

Sandel cites three arguments for affirmative action: (1) "correcting the testing gap"; (2) "compensating for past wrongs"; and (3) "promoting diversity." Arguing against affirmative action, Sandel cites the argument that "racial preferences violate rights."[18]

Sandel considers the first pro argument regarding testing: "One reason for taking race and ethnicity into account is to correct for possible bias in standardized testing."[19] He concludes that "whatever the cause of the testing gap, using standardized tests to predict academic success requires interpreting the scores in light of students' family, social, cultural, and educational backgrounds."[20]

The second argument that he dissects—"compensating for past wrongs"—is more morally complicated. Sandel posits that "if the point is to help the disadvantaged, critics argue, affirmative action should be based on class, not race."[21] He asks rhetorically: "Can we ever have a moral responsibility to redress wrongs committed by a previous generation?"[22]

And third, supporters of affirmative action cite the argument that racial preferences promote diversity on campus. Sandel comments that "the diversity rationale is an argument in the name of the common good—the common good of the school and also of the wider community."[23]

On the other side of the coin, opponents of affirmative action claim that this policy violates an individual's right. The bottom line, Sandel states, may be that "however worthy the goal of a more diverse classroom or more equal society, and however successful affirmative action policies may be in achieving it, using race or ethnicity as a factor in admissions is unfair."[24]

But Sandel introduces a new concept in the debate—"the social purpose of the university."

> Neither the student with high test scores nor the student who comes from a disadvantaged minority group morally deserves to be admitted. . . . Admission is justified insofar as it contributes to the social purpose the university serves.[25]

Sandel grounds his argument for affirmative action on the "philosophies of Kant and Rawls," which he considers "bold attempts to find a basis for justice and rights that is neutral with respect to competing visions of the good life. . . . It is now time to see if their project succeeds."[26] Sandel presents us with a full and nuanced debate over the moral implications of affirmative action.

Moreover, faculty must continue in their role as the academic conscience of the nation as public intellectuals speaking out on questions of moral concern. And they should receive credit for this role in terms of the service component of their faculty responsibilities for consideration for tenure, promotion, and salary.

Russell Jacoby has traced the migration of public intellectuals from the independent scholars of the New York School variety to the academic public intellectual. In his book, *The Last Intellectuals: American Culture in the Age of Academe* (1987), Jacoby bemoans that transition. He writes that "to identify intellectuals with academics . . . implies that to be an intellectual requires a campus address."[27] Another view is that of Diane Ravitch, conservative scholar and public intellectual, who has written on educational topics for a wide range of mass media including the *New York Times* and *Education Week*.

> University faculty spend years acquiring expertise. When they have special knowledge and insight about public issues, it seems to me they have an obligation to add their voice to the public debates, hopefully to enlighten public opinion and enrich the debate. Otherwise the public is denied access to the ideas of those who have spent years studying the topic at hand. To remain silent for fear of offending a funder is a sad abdication of responsibility by a public intellectual or faculty member.[28]

Stanley Aronowitz, a Marxist scholar and public intellectual whom Jacoby identifies as a "transitional figure between the older independent intelligentsia and the rise of the professor," agrees with Ravitch.[29]

> Tenure ought to be an opportunity to step beyond received wisdom and approved knowledge. The political intellectual is a thinker who persists in writing, speaking, and teaching unauthorized ideas.[30]

Michael Bèrubè, a leftist public intellectual and scholar who has written for a number of general publications including the *New York Times*, demurs from those views.

I disagree with your question's implied premise that faculty have an *obligation* to be public intellectuals. Why not let some of them be scholars who specialize in medieval French or ancient Chinese philosophy and who keep to themselves? Nor do I think that they have any obligation to pick up where university presidents have left off. My point is simply that faculty who do try to speak to public matters in public forums should be able to do so without fear of punitive retaliation from their institutions.[31]

STUDENT PROTEST

One variable that cannot be controlled by university administrative policy is student protest. Students can exert enormous power over the life of the university. Gerard J. Degroot and his contributors to the edited volume *Student Protest: The Sixties and After* (1998) give a mixed report on the success of student rebellion. They find that in terms of social protest outside the academy that "most movements do not extend their influence beyond the confines of the campus."[32] The authors claim that students cannot elicit outside societal support for their social protests because they are "seldom treated with reverence or respect by wider society," partly because they are perceived as an "elite minority" that is resented "by those denied the university experience."[33]

But there have been exceptions. The student involvement in the civil rights movement of the 1960s constituted, according to Degroot and his colleagues, "the finest hour of 1960s student radicalism."[34] The reason? Student civil rights workers succeeded because of the support of a "wide constituency [that] existed outside the campus."[35] Especially instrumental in that struggle was the Student Nonviolent Coordinating Committee (SNCC), an offshoot of Martin Luther King Jr.'s parent organization, the Southern Christian Leadership Conference. SNCC inspired white students to form a companion organization: Students for a Democratic Society (SDS), a breakaway organization from the Socialist parent group, League for Industrial Society. SDS became a focal point for student protest against the Vietnam War.

Student rebellion goes back to revolutionary times in the eighteenth century and continues to this day. The peak occurred during the 1960s, when studies show that in the academic year 1969–1970, a full "43 percent of American higher education institutions had some protest."[36] Moreover, the studies indicate that "activism was more likely to occur at institutions which are more selective, and at larger institutions."[37]

Students were more successful in arguing for a "relevant" curriculum, "defined as one that addressed subject matter related to political and social causes."[38] As a result, by the 1970s, black studies programs were created, followed by other ethnic studies and women's studies programs.

A CRISIS OF PURPOSE

The American university is undergoing what Harvard University president Drew Gilpin Faust has called "a crisis of purpose."[39] Writing in the *New York Times* in 2009, Faust predicts "the world economic crisis and the election of Barack Obama will change the future of higher education."[40] She observes that despite the financial constraints now faced by universities, these universities will be called upon by the president to solve social problems.

The problem, according to Faust, is that "American universities have long struggled to meet almost irreconcilable demands."[41] They are being asked to emphasize practical careers yet "pursue knowledge for its own sake; to both add value and question values."[42] Moreover, universities are called upon to "assist immediate national needs."[43]

What makes these differences worse is that the economic crisis "has reinforced America's deep-seated notion that a college degree serves largely instrumental purposes."[44] This "market model" conflicts with the notion that "universities are meant to be producers not just of knowledge but also (often inconvenient) doubt."[45] Faust concludes on an optimistic note. "Human beings need meaning, understanding and perspective as well as jobs," she writes, "the question should not be whether we can afford to believe in such purpose in these times, but whether we can afford not to."[46]

CONCLUSION

We have made the case that universities are moral institutions. They have moral responsibilities to their constituencies—students and faculty—and to their communities and to the nation. There is mounting evidence that these universities are increasingly evolving in a greater moral direction. Despite the national economic recession, there is every indication that these universities will continue on this path.

Education has a political matrix. University presidents have, on average, a short academic tenure. Nevertheless, a strong tradition of moral concern among universities has been established. Students come and go, but faculties have a long academic life span. They may, by default, inherit that moral tradition.

In summary, the American university is imbued with what John Dewey termed the "social spirit."

ENDNOTES

CHAPTER 1: THE MORAL UNIVERSITY

1. John Dewey, *Moral Principles in Education* (Cambridge, MA: The Riverside Press, 1909), 42–43.

2. Dewey, *Moral Principles*, 43.

3. R. S. Peters, *Ethics and Education* (London: Allen & Irwin, 1970), 93.

4. Peters, *Ethics and Education*, 117.

5. Peters, *Ethics and Education*, 304.

6. Stanley Fish, *Save the World on Your Own Time* (New York: Oxford University Press, 2008), 6.

7. Peter Steinfels, "The University's Role in Instilling a Moral Code among Students? None Whatever, Some Argue," *New York Times*, June 19, 2004, http://www.nytimes.com/2004/06/19/us/beliefs-university-s-role-instilling-moral-code-among-students-none-whatever.html?pagewanted=1.

8. Steinfels, "The University's Role in Instilling a Moral Code."

9. Steinfels, "The University's Role in Instilling a Moral Code."

10. Derek Bok, *Our Underachieving Colleges* (Princeton, NJ: Princeton University Press, 2006), 171.

11. Bok, *Our Underachieving Colleges*, 171.

12. Cardinal Newman, *The Idea of a University* (New Haven: Yale University Press, 1996), 76.

13. Newman, *The Idea of the University*, 76.

14. Newman, *The Idea of the University*, 289.

15. Bruce Wilshire, *The Moral Collapse of the University* (Albany: State University of New York Press, 1990), xxiii.

16. Wilshire, *The Moral Collapse of the University*, 58.

17. Wilshire, *The Moral Collapse of the University*, 32.

18. Wilshire, *The Moral Collapse of the University*, xxiv.

19. Wilshire, *The Moral Collapse of the University*, 33.

20. Wilshire, *The Moral Collapse of the University*, 46.

21. Wilshire, *The Moral Collapse of the University*, 47.

22. Edward LeRoy Long Jr., *Higher Education as a Moral Enterprise* (Washington, D.C.: Georgetown University Press, 1992), xiii.

23 Long Jr., *Higher Education as a Moral Enterprise*, xiv.

24. George M. Marsden, *The Soul of the American University* (New York: Oxford University Press, 1993), 3.

25. Marsden, *The Soul of the American University*, 181.

26. Marsden, *The Soul of the American University*, 183.

27. Marsden, *The Soul of the American University*, 191.

28. Marsden, *The Soul of the American University*, 191.

29. Marsden, *The Soul of the American University*, 191.

30. Marsden, *The Soul of the American University*, 193.

31. Marsden, *The Soul of the American University*, 193.

32. Marsden, *The Soul of the American University*, 429.

33. Marsden, *The Soul of the American University*, 429

34. Allan Bloom, *The Closing of the American Mind* (New York: Simon & Schuster, 1987), 25.

35. Bloom, *The Closing of the American Mind*, 25.

36. Bloom, *The Closing of the American Mind*, 325.

37. Bloom, *The Closing of the American Mind*, 26.

38. Bloom, *The Closing of the American Mind*, 344.

39. Bloom, *The Closing of the American Mind*, 344.

40. Roger Kimball, *Tenured Radicals* (New York: Harper & Row, 1990), xv.

41. Kimball, *Tenured Radicals*, xvi.

42. Charles J. Sykes, *ProfScam* (Washington, D.C.: Regency Gateway, 1988), 5.

43. Sykes, *ProfScam*, 6.

44. Sykes, *ProfScam*, 260.

45. Drew Gilpin Faust, "Unleashing Our Most Ambitious Imaginings," October 12, 2007, http://www.president.harvard.edu/speeches/faust.

46. Faust, "Unleashing Our Most Ambitious Imaginings."

47. Jerome Karabel, e-mail to Maurice R. Berube, March 9, 2007.

48. Karabel, e-mail, March 9, 2007.

49. Arthur C. Danto, e-mail to Maurice R. Berube, February 23, 2007.

50. Danto, e-mail.

51. Danto, e-mail.

52. Diane Ravitch, e-mail to Maurice R. Berube, February 16, 2007.

53. Ravitch, e-mail.

54. Henry A. Giroux, "Academic Repression in the First Person," *The Advocate*, February 2007, 1.

55. Michael Bèrubè, e-mail to Maurice R. Berube, February 17, 2007.

56. Jeffrey Glanz, e-mail to Maurice R. Berube, February 16, 2007.

57. Glanz, e-mail.

58. James V. Koch, e-mail to Maurice R. Berube, February 16, 2007.

59. Roseanne Runte, e-mail to Maurice R. Berube, February 16, 2007.

60. Koch, e-mail.

61. Bèrubè, e-mail.

62. Bèrubè, e-mail.

CHAPTER 2: THE MORAL CURRICULUM

1. Derek Bok, *Our Underachieving Colleges* (Princeton, New Jersey: Princeton University Press, 2007), 171.

2. Leslie Wayne, "A Promise to Be Ethical in an Era of Immorality," *New York Times*, May 30, 2009, http://www.nytimes.com/2009/05/30/business/30oath.html.

3. Wayne, "A Promise to Be Ethical."

4. Wayne, "A Promise to Be Ethical."

5. Wayne, "A Promise to Be Ethical."

6. Bok, *Our Underachieving Colleges*, 157.

7. Andre Schlaefli, James R. Rest, and Stephen J. Thomas, "Does Moral Education Improve Moral Judgment? Meta-Analysis of Intervention Studies Using the Defining Issues Test," *Review of Educational Research* 55, no. 263 (fall 1985): 319.

8. Schlaefli, Rest, and Thomas, "Does Moral Education Improve Moral Judgment?" 319.

9. Schlaefli, Rest, and Thomas, "Does Moral Education Improve Moral Judgment?" 319.

10. Matthew J. Mayhew, Tricia A. Seifert, and Ernest T. Pascerella, "Answering the Call: How College Impacts Moral Reasoning Trajectories," (paper presented at the American Educational Association's AERA MDE-SIG Program, San Diego, CA, April 13, 2009).

11. Mayhew, Seifert, and Pascerella, "Answering the Call."

12. Mayhew, Seifert, and Pascerella, "Answering the Call."

13. Mayhew, Seifert, and Pascerella, "Answering the Call."

14. Mayhew, Seifert, and Pascerella, "Answering the Call."

15. Mayhew, Seifert, and Pascerella, "Answering the Call."

16. Robert J. Sternberg, "A New Model for Teaching Ethical Behavior," *The Chronicle of Higher Education*, April 24, 2009, http://chronicle.com/article/A-New-Model-for-Teaching/36202.

17. Sternberg, "A New Model."

18. Sternberg, "A New Model."

19. Christopher Shea, "Michael Sandel Wants to Talk to You about Justice," *The Chronicle of Higher Education*, September 28, 2009, http://chronicle.com/article/michael-sandel-wants-to-talk/48573/?sid=at&utm/28/209.

20. Christopher Shea, "Michael Sandel."

21. Christopher Shea, "Michael Sandel."

22. Christopher Shea, "Michael Sandel."

23. Christopher Shea, "Michael Sandel."

24. Christopher Shea, "Michael Sandel."

25. Michael J. Sandel, *Justice: What's the Right Thing to Do?* (New York: Farrar, Straus and Giroux, 2009).

26. Sandel, *Justice*, 269.

27. New York University Catalog, 2009.

28. New York University Catalog.

29. Bruce Wilshire, e-mail to Maurice R. Berube, July 17, 2007.

30. Wilshire, e-mail.

31. Wilshire, e-mail.

32. Jeffrey Glanz, e-mail to Maurice R. Berube, July 6, 2007.

33. Glanz, e-mail.

34. Glanz, e-mail.

35. Glanz, e-mail.

36. Michael Bèrubè, e-mail to Maurice R. Berube, July 3, 2007.

37. Stanley Aronowitz, e-mail to Maurice R. Berube, July 5, 2007.

38. Diane Ravitch, e-mail to Maurice R. Berube, July 3, 2007.

39. Ravitch, e-mail.

40. Peter Steinfels, interview by Maurice R. Berube, July 15, 2007.

41. Steinfels, interview.

42. Stanley Fish, *Save the World on Your Own Time* (New York: Oxford University Press, 2007), 24.

43. Bok, *Our Underachieving Colleges*, 61.

44. Bok, *Our Underachieving Colleges*, 62.

45. Bok, *Our Underachieving Colleges*, 62.

46. Bok, *Our Underachieving Colleges*, 61–62.

47. Henry Giroux, e-mail to Maurice R. Berube, October 21, 2007.

48. Giroux, e-mail.

49. Michael Bèrubè, *What's Liberal about the Liberal Arts?* (New York: W. W. Norton, 2007), 22.

50. Bèrubè, *What's Liberal about the Liberal Arts?* 23.

51. Bèrubè, *What's Liberal about the Liberal Arts?* 23.

52. Gerald Graff, *Beyond the Culture Wars* (New York: W. W. Norton, 1992), 15.

53. Henry Rosovsky, *The University* (New York: W. W. Norton, 1990), 126.

54. Rosovsky, *The University*, 126–27.

55. Harvard University Catalog, Department of Philosophy, 2009.

56. Stanford University Catalog, Department of Philosophy, 2009.

57. Duke University Catalog, 2009.

58. University of Wisconsin/Madison Catalog, General Education, 2009.

59. University of Wisconsin/Madison Catalog.

60. University of California/Berkeley/Austin Catalog, 2009.

61. University of Texas Catalog, Department of Philosophy, 2009.

62. University of Texas Catalog.

63. Fordham University Catalog, 2009.

64. Virginia Wesleyan Catalog, 2009.

65. Loyola Catalog, 2009.

66. Loyola Catalog, 2009.

67. Loyola Catalog, 2009.

68. Regent University Catalog, 2009.

69. Regent University Catalog.

CHAPTER 3: LEADERSHIP FOR SOCIAL CHANGE

1. Nathan Burchfield, "Teacher Accreditation Agency Drops 'Social Justice,'" June 7, 2006, http://www.cnsnews.com/ViewNation. asp?Page=/Nation/archivee/200606/Nat20060607.

2. Paula Vasley, "Accreditors of Education Schools Drop Controversial 'Social Justice' Term," *The Chronicle of Higher Education*, June 6, 2006.

3. Burchfield, "Teacher Accreditation Agency Drops 'Social Justice.'"

4. Burchfield, "Teacher Accreditation Agency Drops 'Social Justice.'"

5. Burchfield, "Teacher Accreditation Agency Drops 'Social Justice.'"

6. Vaslety, "Accreditors of Education Schools Drop Controversial 'Social Justice' Term."

7. Catherine Marshall and Maricela Oliva, "Building the Capacity of Social Justice Leaders," in *Leadership for Social Justice: Making Revolutions in Education*, ed. Catherine Marshall and Maricela Oliva (New York: Pearson, 2006), 7, 11.

8. Marshall and Oliva, "Building the Capacity of Social Justice Leaders," 1.

9. Marshall and Oliva, "Building the Capacity of Social Justice Leaders," 7.

10. Michael E. Dantley and Linda C. Tillman, "Social Justice and Moral Transformative Leadership, in *Leadership for Social Justice: Making Revolutions in Education*, ed. Catherine Marshall and Maricela Oliva (New York: Pearson, 2006), 16.

11. Dantley and Tillman, "Social Justice and Moral Transformative Leadership," 20.

12. Nelda Cambron-McCabe, "Preparation and Development of School Leaders: Implications for Social Justice Policies," in *Leadership for Social Justice: Making Revolutions in Education*, ed. Catherine Marshall and Maricela Oliva (New York: Pearson, 2006), 121.

13. James McGregor Burns, *Transforming Leadership* (New York: Atlantic Monthly Press, 2003), 2.

14. Katherine S. Mangan, "Leading the Way in Leadership Studies," *The Chronicle of Higher Education*, May 32, 2002, A10.

15. Jepson School of Leadership Cataloge, http://Jepson.richmond. edu/academics/courses/index.htm 4/30/2008.

16. Catherine R. Stimpson and Nina Kressor Cobb, *Women's Studies in the United States* (New York: Ford Foundation, 1986), 42.

17. Michael Bèrubè, *Public Access: Literary Theory and American Cultural Politics* (New York: Verso, 1994), 138.

18. Michael Bèrubè, "What's the Matter with Cultural Studies?" *The Chronicle of Higher Education*, September 14, 2009, http://chronicle.com/article/whats-the-matter-with/48334/?sid=cr&utm_source=cr&utlm.

19. Bèrubè, "What's the Matter with Cultural Studies?"

20. Bèrubè, "What's the Matter with Cultural Studies?"

21. Bèrubè, "What's the Matter with Cultural Studies?"

22. Bèrubè, "What's the Matter with Cultural Studies?"

23. Maurice R. Berube, *Radical Reformers: The Influence of the Left in American Education* (Greenwich, CT: Information Age Publishing, 2004), 5.

24. Berube, *Radical Reformers*, 7.

25. Berube, *Radical Reformers*, 45.

26. Berube, *Radical Reformers*, 45.

27. Berube, *Radical Reformers*, 46.

28. Berube, *Radical Reformers*, 45.

29. Berube, *Radical Reformers*, 45.

30. Berube, *Radical Reformers*, 46.

31. *New York Times*, April 14, 1997.

32. Living Witness. Brochure (Notre Dame, IN: Center for Social Concerns, University Notre Dame, 2008), 6.

33. Trey L. Hill, Jay W. Brandenberger, and George S. Howard, Lasting Effects? A Longitudinal Study of the Impact of Service-Learning Studies in Social Responsibility, Report 8 (Notre Dame, IN: Center for Social Concerns, University of Notre Dame, February 2005), 7.

34. Living Witness, 1; Hill, Brandenberger, and Howard, Lasting Effects? 1.

35. Hill, Brandenberger, and Howard, Lasting Effects? 3.

36. Hill, Brandenberger, and Howard, Lasting Effects? 1.

CHAPTER 4: THE COMMUNITY OF SCHOLARS

1. A. N. Whitehead, *The Aims of Education and Other Essays* (New York: The Macmillan Company, 1959), 10.

2. Derek Bok, *Our Underachieving Colleges* (Princeton, NJ: Princeton University Press 2006), 109.

3. *New York Times*, February 25, 2009, C1.

4. Bok, *Our Underachieving Colleges*, 31.

5. Bok, *Our Underachieving Colleges*, 31.

6. Bok, *Our Underachieving Colleges*, 32.

7. Bok, *Our Underachieving Colleges*, 32.

8. Matthew Miller, "$140,000—And a Bargain," *New York Times Magazine*, June 13, 1999, 48.

9. Miller, "$140,000—And a Bargain," 48.

10. Janet Lyon, e-mail to Maurice R. Berube, February 22, 2009.

11. Stanley Aronowitz, e-mail to Maurine R. Berube, February 23, 2009.

12. Jeffrey Glanz, e-mail to Maurice R. Berube, February 23, 2009.

13. Glanz, e-mail.

14. Glanz, e-mail.

15. James V. Koch, e-mail to Maurice R. Berube, February 23, 2009.

16. Koch, e-mail.

17. Koch, e-mail.

18. Diane Ravitch, e-mail to Maurice R. Berube, February 23, 2009.

19. Anthony T. Kronman, *Education's End* (New Haven: Yale University Press, 2007), 261–63.

20. Ravitch, e-mail.

21. Ravitch, e-mail.

22. Michael Bèrubè, e-mail to Maurice R. Berube, February 23, 2009.

23. Bèrubè, e-mail.

24. Bèrubè, e-mail.

25. Dana Heller, e-mail to Maurice R. Berube, February 26, 2009.

26. Heller, e-mail.

27. Rita Bornstein, "Back in the Spotlight: The College President as Public Intellectual," *Educational Record* 76, no. 4 (fall 1995): 58.

28. Bornstein, "Back in the Spotlight," 58.

29. Virginia Tech Review Panel, The Virginia Tech Review Panel Report (Arlington, VA: Virginia Tech Review Panel, 2008), 2.

30. The Virginia Tech Review Panel Report, 2.

31. The Virginia Tech Review Panel Report, 3.

32. The Virginia Tech Review Panel Report, 3.

33. Bethany L. Waits and Paula Lundberg-Love, "The Impact of Campus Violence on College Students," in *Understanding and Preventing Campus Violence*, ed. Michele A. Paludi (Westport, CT: Praeger, 2008), 51.

34. Michele A. Paludi, "Introduction," in *Understanding and Preventing Campus Violence*, ed. Michele A. Paludi (Westport, CT: Praeger, 2008), xvii.

35. Bok, *Our Underachieving Colleges*, 149.

36. Bok, *Our Underachieving Colleges*, 150.

37. William G. Bowen and Derek Bok, *The Shape of the River* (Princeton, NJ: Princeton University Press, 1998), xxvii–xxix, 55–57.

38. K. Anthony Appiah and Amy Gutmann, *Color Conscious: The Political Morality of Race* (Princeton, NJ: Princeton University Press, 1996), 139.

39. Appiah and Gutmann, *Color Conscious*, 139.

CHAPTER 5: GENDER BIAS IN ACADEMIA

1. Myra Sadker and David Sadker, *Failing at Fairness: How Our Schools Cheat Girls* (New York: Simon & Schuster, 1994), 50.

2. Sadker and Sadker, *Failing at Fairness*, 166.

3. *Boston Globe*, January 1, 2005, 1.

4. Anne M. Schoening, "Women and Tenure: Closing the Gap," *Journal of Women in Educational Leadership* 7, no. 2: 77–92.

5. Schoening, "Women and Tenure," 77.

6. Schoening, "Women and Tenure," 78.

7. Schoening, "Women and Tenure," 78.

8. Schoening, "Women and Tenure," 78.

9. Schoening, "Women and Tenure," 80.

10. Schoening, "Women and Tenure," 80.

11. Schoening, "Women and Tenure," 80.

12. Schoening, "Women and Tenure," 82.

13. Schoening, "Women and Tenure," 82.

14. Mary Ann Mason, "Title IX Includes Maternal Discrimination," *The Chronicle of Higher Education*, November 19, 2009, http://www.chronicle.com/article/title-IX-includes-maternal/49149/?sid=at/utm_sourceAT&U.

15. Mason, "Title IX Includes Maternal Discrimination."

16. Katherine Hanson, Vivian Guilfoy, and Sarita Pillai, *More Than Title IX: How Equity in Education Has Shaped the Nation* (New York: Rowman & Littlefield, 2009), 39.

17. Hanson, Guilfoy, and Pillai, *More Than Title IX*, 166.

18. *The Chronicle of Higher Education*, February 20, 2009, http://unweb.hwwilsonweb.com.proxy.lib.odu.edu/hww/results/get-results.jhtml?

19. *The Chronicle of Higher Education*, February 20, 2009.

20. *The Chronicle of Higher Education*, February 20, 2009.

21. Mason, "Title IX Includes Maternal Discrimination."

22. National Organization for Women, press release, January 20, 2005.

23. National Organization for Women, press release.

24. Hanson, Guilfoy, and Pillai, *More Than Title IX*, 84.

25. Kerry K. Karukstis, "Women in Science, Beyond the Research University: Overlooked and Undervalued," *The Chronicle of Higher Education*, June 29, 2009, A23.

26. Ajda Kahueci, Sherry A. Southerland, and Penny J. Gilmer, "Retaining Undergraduate Women in Science, Mathematics and Engineering," *Journal of College Science Teaching* 36, no. 3 (November/December 2006): 34.

27. Kahueci, Southerland, and Gilmer, "Retaining Undergraduate Women in Science, Mathematics and Engineering," 38.

28. http://www.awis.org.

CHAPTER 6: THE UNIVERSITY AND THE NATION

1. Henry A. Giroux, *The University in Chains: Confronting the Military-Industrial-Academic Complex* (Boulder, CO: Paradigm Publishers, 2007), 203.

2. Clark Kerr, *The Uses of the University* (New York: Harper & Row, 1966), 86.

3. Giroux, *The University in Chains*, 13.

4. Giroux, *The University in Chains*, 15.

5. Giroux, *The University in Chains*, 14.

6. Giroux, *The University in Chains*, 15.

7. Jennifer Washburn, *University, Inc.: The Corporate Corruption of American High Education* (New York: Basic Books, 2005), 42.

8. Washburn, *University, Inc.*, 43.

9. Stuart W. Leslie, *The Cold War and American Science: The Military-Industrial-Academic Complex at MIT and Stanford* (New York: Columbia University Press, 1993), 1.

10. Leslie, *The Cold War and American Science*, 2.

11. Leslie, *The Cold War and American Science*, 9.

12. Leslie, *The Cold War and American Science*, 3.

13. Leslie, *The Cold War and American Science*, 235.

14. Leslie, *The Cold War and American Science*, 243.

15. Leslie, *The Cold War and American Science*, 233.

16. Leslie, *The Cold War and American Science*, 233.

17. Leslie, *The Cold War and American Science*, 235.

18. Leslie, *The Cold War and American Science*, 241.

19. Leslie, *The Cold War and American Science*, 235.

20. James Ridgeway, *The Closed Corporation: American Universities in Crisis* (New York: Random House, 1968), 5.

21. Ridgeway, *The Closed Corporation*, 5.

22. Ridgeway, *The Closed Corporation*, back cover.

23. Giroux, *The University in Chains*, 22.

24. Giroux, *The University in Chains*, 53.

25. Giroux, *The University in Chains*, 57 (emphasis added).

26. Giroux, *The University in Chains*, 206.

27. Giroux, *The University in Chains*, 206.

28. Washburn, *University, Inc.*, ix.

29. Washburn, *University, Inc.*, x.

30. Washburn, *University, Inc.*, x.

31. Washburn, *University, Inc.*, 2–3.

32. Washburn, *University, Inc.*, 3.

33. Washburn, *University, Inc.*, 225.

34. Washburn, *University, Inc.*, 225.

35. Washburn, *University, Inc.*, 225.

36. Giroux, *The University in Chains*, 105.

37. Giroux, *The University in Chains*, 111.

38. James V. Koch, e-mail to Maurice R. Berube, May 14, 2009.

39. Michael Bèrubè, e-mail to Maurice R. Berube, May 14, 2009.

40. Michael Bèrubè, e-mail to Maurice R. Berube, May 14, 2009.

41. Jeffrey Glanz, e-mail to Maurice R. Berube, May 14, 2009.

42. Jeffrey Glanz, e-mail.

43. Peter Steinfels, e-mail to Maurice R. Berube, May 19, 2009.

44. Peter Steinfels, e-mail.

45. Peter Steinfels, e-mail.

46. Peter Steinfels, e-mail.

47. Christopher J. Lucas, *American Higher Education: A History* (New York: St. Martins Griffin, 1994), 237–38.

CHAPTER 7: TOWARD A MORAL UNIVERSITY

1. Philip G. Altbach, e-mail to Maurice R. Berube, September 15, 2009.

2. Sophie Body-Gendrot, e-mail to Maurice R. Berube, September 18, 2009.

3. Francesca Gobbo, e-mail to Maurice R. Berube, September 19, 2009.

4. Altbach, e-mail.

5. Altbach, e-mail.

6. Maurice R. Berube, *The Urban University in America* (Westport, CT: Greenwood Press, 1978), 51.

7. Berube, *The Urban University in America*, 47.

8. Evan S. Dobelle, "Saviors of Our Cities," abstract, October 2009.

9. Dobelle, "Saviors of Our Cities," abstract.

10. Dobelle, "Saviors of Our Cities," abstract.

11. Evan S. Dobelle, "Saviors of Our Cities: Survey of Best College and University Civic Partnerships," full report, October 2009.

12. Dobelle, "Saviors of Our Cities, full report.

13. Dobelle, "Saviors of Our Cities," abstract.

14. Dobelle, "Saviors of Our Cities," abstract.

15. Dobelle, "Saviors of Our Cities," abstract.

16. Old Dominion University, press release, November 2, 2009.

17. Old Dominion University, press release.

18. Michael J. Sandel, *Justice: What's the Right Thing to Do?* (New York: Farrar, Straus and Giroux, 2009), 169–73.

19. Sandel, *Justice*, 169.

20. Sandel, *Justice*, 169.

21. Sandel, *Justice*, 170.

22. Sandel, *Justice*, 170.

23. Sandel, *Justice*, 171.

24. Sandel, *Justice*, 173.

25. Sandel, *Justice*, 174.

26. Sandel, *Justice*, 183.

27. Russell Jacoby, *The Last Intellectuals: American Culture in the Age of Academe* (New York: Basic Books, 1987), 220.

28. Diane Ravitch, e-mail to Maurice R. Berube, October 25, 2009.

29. Stanley Aronowitz, e-mail to Maurice R. Berube, October 25, 2009.

30. Aronowitz, e-mail.

31. Michael Bèrubè, e-mail to Maurice R. Berube, October 26, 2009.

32. Gerard J. Degroot, *Student Protest: The Sixties and After* (New York: Longman, 1998), 733.

33. Degroot, *Student Protest*, 6.

34. Degroot, *Student Project*, 9.

35. Degroot, *Student Project*, 9.

36. Degroot, *Student Project*, 29.

37. Degroot, *Student Project*, 29.

38. Degroot, *Student Project*, 154.

39. Drew Gilpin Faust, "The University's Crisis of Purpose," *New York Times Book Review*, September 6, 2009, 19.

40. Drew Gilpin Faust, "The University's Crisis of Purpose," 19.

41. Drew Gilpin Faust, "The University's Crisis of Purpose," 19.

42. Drew Gilpin Faust, "The University's Crisis of Purpose," 19.

43. Drew Gilpin Faust, "The University's Crisis of Purpose," 19.

44. Drew Gilpin Faust, "The University's Crisis of Purpose," 19.

45. Drew Gilpin Faust, "The University's Crisis of Purpose," 19.

46. Drew Gilpin Faust, "The University's Crisis of Purpose," 19.

SELECTED
BIBLIOGRAPHY

Appiah, K. Anthony, and Amy Gutmann. *Color Conscious: The Political Morality of Race*. Princeton, NJ: Princeton University Press, 1996.

Berube, Maurice R. *The Urban University in America*. Westport, CT: Greenwood Press, 1978.

——. *Radical Reformers: The Influence of the Left in American Education*. Greenwich, CT: Information Age Publishing, 2004.

Bèrubè, Michael. *Public Access: Literary Theory and American Cultural Politics*. New York: Verso, 1994.

——. *What's Liberal about the Liberal Arts?* New York: W. W. Norton, 2007.

——. "What's the Matter with Cultural Studies?" *The Chronicle of Higher Education*, September 14, 2009. http://chronicle.com/article/whats-the-matter-with/48334/?sid=cr&utm_source=cr&utlm.

Bloom, Allan. *The Closing of the American Mind*. New York: Simon & Schuster, 1987.

Bok, Derek. *Our Underachieving Colleges*. Princeton, NJ: Princeton University Press, 2006.

Bornstein, Rita. "Back in the Spotlight: The College President as Public Intellectual," *Educational Record* 76, no. 4 (fall 1995): 56–62.

Bowen, William G., and Derek Bok. *The Shape of the River*. Princeton, NJ: Princeton University Press, 1998.

Burns, James McGregor. *Transforming Leadership*. New York: Atlantic Monthly Press, 2003.

Degroot, Gerard J., ed. *Student Protest: The Sixties and After*. New York: Longman, 1998.

Dewey, John. *Moral Principles in Education*. Cambridge, MA: The Riverside Press, 1909.

Dobelle, Evan S. "Saviors of Our Cities: Survey of Best Colleges and University Civic Partnerships." Abstract. October 2009.

——. "Saviors of Our Cities: Survey of Best College and University Civic Partnerships," Full report. October 2009.

Faust, Drew Gilpin, "Unleashing Our Most Ambitious Imaginings." October 12, 2007. http://www.president.harvard.edu/speeches/faust.

——. "The University's Crisis of Purpose." *New York Times Book Review*, September 6, 2009.

Fish, Stanley. *Save the World on Your Own Time*. New York: Oxford University Press, 2008.

Giroux, Henry A. "Academic Repression in the First Person." *The Advocate*, February 2007.

——. *The University in Chains: Confronting the Military-Industrial-Academic Complex*. Boulder, CO: Paradigm Publishers, 2007.

Graff, Gerald. *Beyond the Culture Wars*. New York: W. W. Norton, 1992.

Hanson, Katherine, Vivian Guilfoy, and Sarita Pillai. *More Than Title IX: How Equity in Education Has Shaped the Nation*. New York: Rowman & Littlefield, 2009.

Hill, Trey L. Jay W. Brandenberger, and George S. Howard. Lasting Effects? A Longitudinal Study of the Impact of Service-Learning Studies in Social Responsibility. Report 8. Notre Dame, IN: Center for Social Concerns, University of Notre Dame, February 2005.

Jacoby, Russell. *The Last Intellectuals: American Culture in the Age of Academe*. New York: Basic Books, 1987.

Kahueci, Ajda, Sherry A. Southerland, and Penny J. Gilmer. "Retaining Undergraduate Women in Science, Mathematics and Engineering." *Journal of College Science Teaching* 36, no. 3 (November/December 2006): 34–38.

Karukstis, Kerry K. "Women in Science, Beyond the Research University: Overlooked and Undervalued." *The Chronicle of Higher Education*, June 29, 2009.

Kerr, Clark. *The Uses of the University*. New York: Harper and Row, 1966.

Kimball, Roger. *Tenured Radicals*. New York: Harper & Row, 1990.

Kronman, Anthony T. *Education's End*. New Haven: Yale University Press, 2007.

Leslie, Stuart L. *The Cold War and American Science: The Military-Industrial-Academic Complex at MIT and Stanford*. New York: Columbia University Press, 1993.

Long, Edward Leroy, Jr. *Higher Education as a Moral Enterprise*. Washington, D.C.: Georgetown University Press, 1992.

Lucas, Christopher J. *American Higher Education: A History*. New York: St. Martins Griffin, 1994.

Marsden, George M. *The Soul of the American University*. New York: Oxford University Press, 1993.

Marshall, Catherine, and Maricela Oliva, eds. *Leadership for Social Justice: Making Revolutions in Education*. New York: Pearson, 2006.

Mason, Mary Ann. "Title IX Includes Maternal Discrimination." *The Chronicle of Higher Education*, November 19, 2009. http://www.chronicle.com/article/title-IX-includes-maternal/49149/?sid=at/utm_sourceAT&U.

Mayhew, Matthew J., Tricia A. Seifert, and Ernest T. Pascerella. "Answering the Call: How College Impacts Moral Reasoning Trajectories." Paper presented at the American Educational Association's AERA MDE-SIG Program, San Diego, CA, April 13, 2009.

Miller, Matthew. "$140,000—And a Bargain." *New York Times Magazine*, June 13, 1999.

Newman, Cardinal. *The Idea of a University*. New Haven: Yale University Press, 1996.

Paludi, Michele A., ed. *Understanding and Preventing Campus Violence*. Westport, CT: Praeger, 2008.

Peters, R. S. *Ethics and Education*. London: Allen & Irwin, 1970.

Ridgeway, James. *The Closed Corporation: American Universities in Crisis*. New York: Random House, 1968.

Rosovsky, Henry. *The University*. New York: W. W. Norton, 1990.

Sadker, Myra, and David Sadker. *Failing at Fairness: How Our Schools Cheat Girls*. New York: Simon & Schuster, 1994.

Sandel, Michael J. *Justice: What's the Right Thing to Do?* New York: Farrar, Straus and Giroux, 2009.

Schlaefli, Andre, James R. Rest, and Stephen J. Thomas. "Does Moral Education Improve Moral Judgment? Meta-Analysis of Intervention Studies Using the Defining Issues Test." *Review of Educational Research* 55, no. 263 (fall 1985): 319–52.

Shea, Christopher. "Michael Sandel Wants to Talk to You about Justice." *The Chronicle of Higher Education,* September 28, 2009. http://chronicle.com/article/michael-sandel-wants-to-talk/48573/ ?sid=at&utm/28/209.

Shoening, Anne M. "Women and Tenure: Closing the Gap." *Journal of Women in Educational Leadership* (April 2009): 7, no. 2: 77–92.

Steinfels, Peter. "The University's Role in Instilling a Moral Code among Students? None Whatever, Some Argue." *New York Times,* June 19, 2004. http://www.nytimes.com/2004/06/19/us/beliefs-university-s-role-instilling-moral-code-among-students-none-whatever.html?pagewanted=1.

Sternberg, Robert J. "A New Model for Teaching Ethical Behavior." *The Chronicle of Higher Education,* April 24, 2009. http://chronicle.com/article/A-New-Model-for-Teaching/36202.

Stimpson, Catherine R., with Nina Kressor Cobb. *Women's Studies in the United States.* New York: Ford Foundation, 1986.

Sykes, Charles J. *ProfScam.* Washington, D.C.: Regency Gateway, 1988.

Virginia Tech Review Panel. The Virginia Tech Review Panel Report. Arlington, VA: 2008.

Washburn, Jennifer. *University, Inc.: The Corporate Corruption of American Higher Education.* New York: Basic Books, 2005.

Wayne, Leslie. "A Promise to Be Ethical in an Era of Immorality." *New York Times,* May 30, 2009. http://www.nytimes.com/2009/05/30/business/30oath.html.

Whitehead, A. N. *The Aims of Education and Other Essays.* New York: The MacMillan Company, 1959.

Wilshire, Bruce. *The Moral Collapse of the University.* Albany: State University of New York Press, 1990.

INDEX

INDEX

ABOUT THE AUTHORS

Maurice R. Berube is eminent scholar emeritus of education from Old Dominion University.

Clair T. Berube is assistant professor of science education at Hampton University.

They are also the authors of *The End of School Reform* (Rowman & Littlefield, 2007).

Breinigsville, PA USA
11 May 2010
237779BV00002B/2/P